The World Will Long Remember

This guide generally follows the Gettysburg National Park Service route; however, that route changes periodically as do the stops. To assist the visitor around the battlefield, a map of the entire area and the stops listed are shown on the map to the right. In addition, notations on the maps within indicate the appropriate roads, routes and stop locations. There are no park markers for the stops suggested herein; however, where applicable the corresponding National Park Stop is indicated.

1. McPherson's Ridge; Reynold's Ave.
2. John Burn's Monument; Stone/Merdith's Ave.
3. Railroad Cut; Wadsworth's Ave.
4. Oak Ridge; Doubleday's Ave.
5. Forney's Field; Buford's Ave.
6. Lutheran Theological Seminary; Seminary Ave.
7. North Carolina Monument; West Confederate Ave.
8. Virginia Monument; West Confederate Ave.
9. Warfield Ridge; West Confederate Ave.
10. Little Round Top; Sykes' Ave.
    a. 20th Maine Monument, southeastern slope.
    b. 140th New York Monument, northwestern slope.
11. Devil's Den;
    a. East-Devil's Den, near 4th Maine Monument.
    b. West-Devil's Den, near 4th New York Battery Monument
12. Wheatfield
13. Peach Orchard; Wheatfield Road/Sickles' Ave.
14. The battle for Emmitsburg Road; Sickles' Ave./United States Ave.
15. Trostle's Farm; United States Ave.
16. Father Corby's Monument; Hancock Ave.
17. First Minnesota Monument; Hancock Ave.
18. Spangler's Spring; Slocum Ave.
19. Culp's Hill, 137th New York Monument; Slocum Ave./William's Ave.
20. East-Cemetery Hill; Baltimore Pike
21. Jennie Wade's story; Baltimore Pike
22. The cannonade, July 3; Pleasonton's Ave./Hancock's Ave.
23. Cemetery Ridge: "Pickett's Charge;" Hancock's Ave.
    a. 13th, 14th, 16th Vermont Monuments.
    b. Cowan's Battery, First Independent New York Artillery
    c. "The Angle"
    d. First Rhode Island Battery "A."
    e. Bryan's Farm
24. National Cemetery, Soldier's National Monument

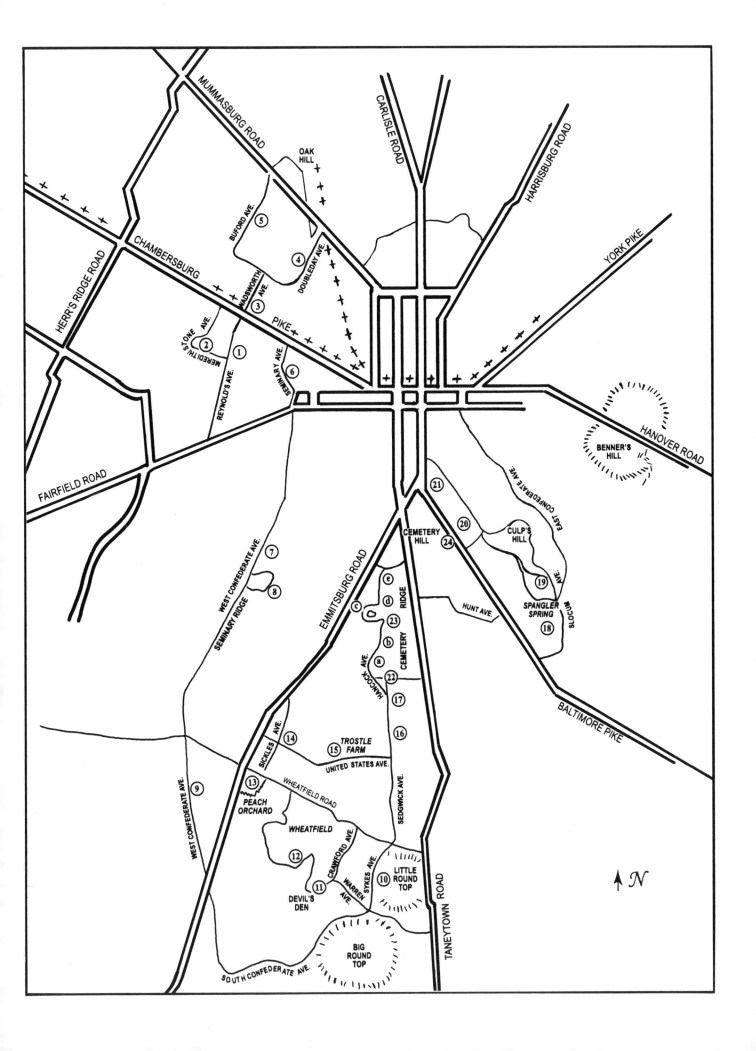

A Guide to
The Battle of Gettysburg

The World Will Long Remember

by
JoAnna M. McDonald

 White Mane Publishing Company, Inc.

This White Mane Publishing Company, Inc. publication
was printed by
Beidel Printing House, Inc.
63 West Burd Street
Shippensburg, PA 17257-0152 USA

In respect for the scholarship contained herein, the acid-free paper used in this book meets the guidelines for permanence and durability of the Committee on Production Guidelines for Book Longevity of the Council on Library Resources.

For a complete list of available publications
please write
White Mane Publishing Company, Inc.
P.O. Box 152
Shippensburg, PA 17257-0152 USA

Library of Congress Cataloging-in-Publication Data

McDonald, JoAnna M., 1970-
        The world will long remember : a guide to the Battle of Gettysburg
/ by JoAnna M. McDonald.
            p.   cm.
        Includes bibliographical references and index.
        ISBN 1-57249-000-4.--ISBN 1-57249-127-2 (pbk.)
        1. Gettysburg (Pa.), Battle of, 1863. 2. Gettysburg National
Military Park (Pa.)--Guidebooks. I. Title.
        E475.53.M473 1996
        973.7'349--dc20   96-9807
                                                              CIP

To the
loved ones
left behind.

Table of Contents

* Indicates Optional Site

* Indicates Optional Site

Acknowledgements

I wish to thank my parents, Norman and Barbara, and grandparents, Frances and Don, who understood and supported my interest in military history. They took me to Civil War sites and introduced me to Civil War books, journals and magazines, and subsidized my projects. My mother acted as secretary and novice reader/editor for all the drafts of this manuscript. I want to thank also my sisters, other family members and friends who, through the years, allowed me to "guide" them around the Gettysburg National Park. They showed great patience and tact and did not discourage even the child of ten. Jeff Wood, owner and proprietor of the Whistlestop Book Stores in Carlisle and Gettysburg, persuaded me to submit my manuscript for publication and encouraged me through the long process.

This manuscript could not have been completed, however, without the cooperation and assistance of several academic institutions. I began this work as a student at Dickinson College under the tutelage of Professor Charles Jarvis who provided constructive criticism and encouragement. The secretaries of Denny Hall were also very supportive and kind throughout the long process of development, and the staff of the Spahr Library exhibited forbearance concerning my overdue books.

Shippensburg University professors Jerry Butcher, Paul Gill, and Dana V. Sadarananda approved my use of this project as partial credit toward my Masters Degree and provided excellent editorial comments. My advisor, Dennis Castelli, was helpful as well.

But the most important institution was the Military History Institute, U.S. Army War College, Carlisle Barracks, Carlisle, Pennsylvania. The reference staff—Louise Arnold-Friend, John Slonaker, Dennis Vetock, Kathleen Gildersleeve, and Michelle Stalnecker—provided both guidance and friendship. Dr. Richard Sommers, David Keough, and Pamela Cheney, aided me in the archives department. And the boys in the photo archives, Michael Winey and Randy Hackenburg, put up with me for several years, and still allow me to use the facilities! In addition, Mr. Winey acted as my fact-editor and photo consultant.

I would like also to express my gratitude to Professor Jay Luvaas. When I was a freshman at Dickinson, he conducted a military history class as a visiting professor. Recognizing my great interest in the subject, he waived the pre-requisite and allowed me to take the upper-level course, and our association began. While a graduate student at Shippensburg, he invited me to attend his seminars at the U.S. Army War College. His secretary, Chris Hockensmith, was able to accomplish the impossible and as a civilian graduate student I was accepted as a member of several of Professor Luvaas' classes. With his trust and teaching to further ignite my interest in military history, he instilled in me the courage and dedication to go forward. I am privileged to count Jay Luvaas as my mentor and friend.

Lastly, Wayne Motts also made several excellent suggestions for improving the text. I thank the staff and owners of White Mane Publishing Company and you, my readers, for giving this book a chance.

The American Civil War was one of the most devastating and trying times in our nation's history. In a mere four years, April 12, 1861 to April 9, 1865, 3,750,000 Americans enlisted into the Confederate and Union armies.[1] Of this number 623,026 died, (includes all causes) and 471,427 were wounded in battle.[2]

The Battle of Gettysburg is known as the greatest battle fought on the North American continent. The Civil War was in its second year; both sides had sustained heavy casualties. From July 1-3, 1863, 160,000 soldiers from the Army of the Potomac (Union) and the Army of Northern Virginia (Confederates) clashed near the small, peaceful town in south-central Pennsylvania. In that short time 40,322 Americans were killed or wounded, and another 10,000 were captured or missing.

To better comprehend those numbers one should visit the Gettysburg National Military Park itself. However, this book provides a study of that battle for the reader, whether on site or at home. Several guides are readily available, but there remains the need for a clear, introductory narrative to the action which can be used by both the novice and Civil War historian. Therefore, many of the smaller struggles which essentially made up that larger conflict have been defined herein.

Lieutenant Frank Haskell

With the aid of photographs, maps, first-hand accounts and secondary sources, the reader will be able to envision that massive, destructive battle which occurred over 130 years ago. They will read the words and meet the personalities of fathers, brothers, sons, husbands and lovers— from generals to privates who fought and died here.

This study, however, is not an exhaustive account; it attempts only to supply specific day-by-day details of the conflict. Even those involved could tell only of their own part in the story. As Lieutenant Frank Haskell, a Union staff officer at Gettysburg, stated:

> [A] full account of the battle as it was will never, can never be made. Who could sketch the changes, the constant shifting of the bloody panorama? It is not possible.[3]

The Organization of the Armies

To appreciate the complexities of the battle it is necessary to understand the organization of both armies: the standard military tactics used, the weapons, clothing and general background of the struggle.

Each army consisted of, in order of size, corps, divisions, brigades, regiments and companies; yet, they were organized in different ways.

The Army of Northern Virginia had, by the time of Gettysburg, been reorganized into three infantry corps, each consisting of 21,000-22,000 men.[4]

ARMY OF NORTHERN VIRGINIA, JULY 1, 1863

	Corps	Divisions	Numbers	Brigades No. of Regts. in each	Artl
I	Longstreet 21,400	McLaws	7,300 (429)	Kershaw, 5; Barksdale, 4; Semmes, 4; Wofford, 4.	
		Pickett	5,400 (360)	Garnett, 5; Kemper, 5; Armistead, 5.	
		Hood	7,700 (428)	Law, 5; Robertson, 4; Anderson, 5; Benning, 4.	
		Artillery	1,000		84
II	Ewell 22,200	Early	6,300 (370)	Hays, 5; Smith, 3; Hoke, 3; Gordon, 6.	
		Johnson	6,300 (332)	Steuart, 5; Walker, 5; Nicholls, 5; Jones, 6.	
		Rodes	8,600 (390)	Daniel, 5; Doles, 4; Iverson, 4; Ramseur, 4; O'Neal, 5.	
		Artillery	1,000		84
III	A. P. Hill 22,000	Anderson	7,200 (343)	Wilcox, 5; Wright, 4; Mahone, 5; Perry, 3; Posey, 4.	
		Heth	7,600 (447)	Pettigrew, 4; Brockenborough, 4; Archer, 5; Davis, 4.	
		Pender	6,200 (326)	Perrin, 5; Lane, 5; Thomas, 4; Scales, 5.	
		Artillery	1,000		80
Cav.	10,000	Stuart	10,000 (416)	Hampton, 6; Robertson, 2; Jones, 3; F. Lee, 5. Jenkins, 4; W.H.F. Lee, 4. Artillery	24
Tot.	75,600		75,600 (372)		272

(The numbers in parentheses represent the average strength of an infantry regiment.) Each corps was then divided into three divisions (5,000-7,000 men), with three or four brigades (1,500-2,000 troops) in each division. Four or five regiments then made up each brigade. A full regiment numbered 1,000; however, by 1863, the regimental numbers were greatly reduced. This, in turn, affected the size of the entire organization respectively.

The Army of the Potomac was arranged in a different manner. The army was composed of seven infantry corps (10,000-13,000 men) with three small divisions (3,000-5,000 soldiers) creating a corps, and two-to-four brigades constituting a division, while four-to-eight regiments established a brigade. The Union regiments had also suffered from heavy campaigning and were not at full strength.

ARMY OF THE POTOMAC, JULY 1, 1863[5]

					Artl 110
	Provost Gd. Artillery Res.		2,600 2,600		
	Corps	Divisions		Brigades No. of Regts. in each	23
I	Reynolds 11,900 (573)	Wadsworth Robinson Doubleday	4,100 4,100 3,700	Meredith, 5; Cutler, 6. Paul, 5; Baxter, 6. Rowley, 4; Stone 3; Stannard, 3.	
II	Hancock 12,200 (293)	Caldwell Gibbon Hays	4,500 4,000 3,700	Cross, 4; Kelley, 2; Zook, 4; Brooke, 5. Harrow, 4; Webb, 4; Hall, 5 Carroll, 4; Smyth, 4.5; Willard, 3.4.	24
III	Sickles 11,300 (289)	Birney Humphreys	5,800 5,500	Graham, 6; Ward, 8; De Trobriand, 5. Carr, 6; Brewster, 6; Burling, 6.	30
V	Sykes 12,200 (334)	Barnes Ayres Crawford	4,700 3,900 3,600	Tilton, 4; Sweitzer, 4; Vincent, 4. Day, 3; Burbank, 3; Weed, 4. McCandless, 4; Fisher, 5.	26
VI	Sedgwick 13,800 (367)	Wright Howe Newton	4,700 4,000 5,100	Torbert, 4; Bartlett, 4; Russell, 4. Grant, 5; Neill, 5. Shaler, 5; Eustis, 4; Weaton, 4.	48
XI	Howard 10,300 (373)	Barlow Steinwehr Schurz	3,200 3,200 3,900	Von Gilsa, 4; Ames, 4. Coster, 4; Smith, 4. Schimmelfennig, 5; Krzyzanovski, 5.	26
XII	Slocum (William's) 10,500 (351)	Ruger Geary Indep.	4,100 5,300 1,100	McDougall, 6; Colgrove, 5. Candy, 6; Kane, 3; Greene, 5. Lockwood, 3.	20
Cav.	Pleasonton 13,900 (445)	Buford Gregg Kilpatrick	5,800 4,300 3,800	Gamble, 3; Devin, 4; Merritt, 5. McIntosh, 5; Gregg, 4. Farnsworth, 4; Custer, 4.	50
Tot.	96,100 (330)		101,300		357

3

It is important to note these organizational differences. Overall, on the first day two Confederate corps equaling 28,700 were engaged against two Union corps numbering 20,000 troops. The second day 34,000 Confederates clashed with 33,000 Yankees. On the third day the armies were even at 20,000 and 20,000. Yet at specific fields of battle the Confederates had more strength—such as at Little Round Top on the second day of fighting when the 20th Maine (360) met the 15th Alabama (499). One can readily see that two Confederate corps engaging two Union corps at times presented overwhelming odds. Since the Confederate corps were larger, so too, were their subordinate units. Nevertheless, within the larger battle, smaller conflicts raged between brigades and regiments with the numerical advantage see-sawing. One would assume that the larger side had a better chance of winning. However, if a mismatch occurred on the battlefield, two things were possible: The smaller unit would be routed, or, out of sheer desperation and competent leadership, could overcome the larger force. During the tour the visitor will see examples of both.

Military Tactics of the 19th Century

During the 19th Century shoulder-to-shoulder tactics continued to be the standard military form for fighting. Military historian, Professor Russell Weigley, explained:

> [T]he tactical means wherewith to strike the enemy had to be the close-order infantry assault; no other method of attack permitted adequate communication among the attacking troops or could hope to muster enough weight to break the enemy's lines and achieve Napoleonic results.[6]

The sound of thousands of weapons being fired was deafening, and the smoke was blinding. A commanding officer had to stay close to the front lines for purposes of communication, in order to direct or lead his men to the desired location. And many generals and subordinate officers strongly affirmed heroic leadership. They did not simply order their men into battle they led them. This display of bravery encouraged the private soldier into the fray. However, due to that heroic leadership numerous officers at Gettysburg—both Northerners and Southerners—were either killed or wounded.

Also, an infantryman could only fire two or three shots per minute. To produce an adequate

A Company from 139th Pennsylvania. Although formed for inspection, this photograph shows the "close-order" deployment used during battle.

volume of fire the troops were deployed in close-order linear formations to deliver a powerful blow to their front. Consequently, their flanks were weak and vulnerable to an enemy's counter-attack.

In addition to aiding in communications and effective fire power, the armies used the close order formation because it was the standard tactic taught at West Point, where many of the commanding officers had been trained. Having studied Napoleonic tactics, they had learned from them to form their attacks in a two-rank line, with a frontage of about 200-500 men (depending on the size of the unit). Fifty men walked ahead of their regiment acting as skirmishers. Half of the attackers provided covering fire, while the other half rushed forward to fire at the enemy. Using this leap-frog approach, the attackers hoped to punch a hole in the opposing line, rush through the gap and meet the enemy on his flanks.[7]

If attacking head-on was too difficult and useless, both armies attempted to out maneuver the opposing force in a tactic called flanking. One will discover at Gettysburg that hitting the opponent's sides, both on the grand and smaller scale, was accomplished throughout the battle, a tactic most effective in inflicting heavy casualties. Historian Major General J.F.C. Fuller explained by making the comparison of two men fighting with their fists. In order to win, the fighters must think, guard, move and hit. At the beginning of the bout the individual assumes a defensive attitude. When he has measured and studied his adversary he moves secretly, under cover of his defense, to assume the offense. He will concentrate his blows at the weakest points of his enemy, either left or right jaw or his opponent's mid-section; and throughout the fight he will try to surprise his opponent, catch him off-guard, and knock him out.[8] If a unit was flanked, the entire battle line could quickly be shattered and the remaining soldiers forced to retreat. Once one unit fell the rest soon followed, unless the army could secure its flank.

HEADQUARTERS

General Lee's headquarters on the Chambersburg Pike.

The stone house is on your left before Stop 6.

Major General Meade's headquarters near Taneytown Road.

Look for this house at Stop 23d.

Weapons at Gettysburg

INFANTRY

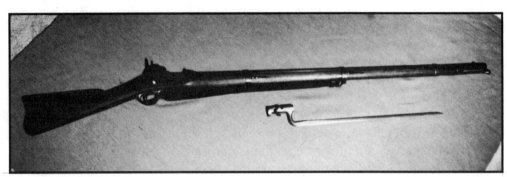

Springfield Rifle Musket Model of 1861 with bayonet.
Private Collection

The primary infantry weapon of 19th century warfare was the smoothbore musket which had a range of only a few hundred yards. However, by 1863 most infantry soldiers at Gettysburg were armed with muzzle-loading rifles.

Along with the rifle came a new, more destructive bullet, the Minié ball, which was not ball-shaped. This bullet was elongated, pointed at the front and recessed at the base, made of soft lead. When the bullet was rammed down the barrel the edges bit into the rifling grooves, fitting snugly within the barrel. On firing, the force of the explosion expanded the bullet into the rifling grooves which gave the projectile a spinning motion as it exited the rifle. Therefore, the bullet was more accurate and had a longer range.

Minié ball cartridge

When the rifle was tested in the 1850s by Cadmus M. Wilcox, he reported that a "well-directed rifle fire was 'irresistible' at 600 yards and still destructive at 1,000 or 1,200 yards."[9] The rifle above had an effective range of 300-400 yards and could kill at 1,000 yards.

The process of loading the weapon was quite cumbersome. The soldier tore the tail of the cartridge with his teeth, poured the black powder into the barrel, and then rammed the ball down with his ramrod. Next he cocked the hammer back, put a percussion cap on the nipple, which was just below the hammer, took aim and fired. A well-trained soldier could make three shots per minute; however, under the excitement of battle this number often was unrealistic. The soldier could also fix a bayonet on his rifle. This weapon was used during hand-to-hand combat. It was somewhat crude but effective.

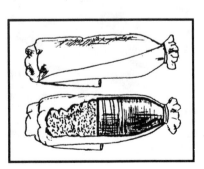

Cartridge

An infantryman tears the cartridge with his teeth.

Infantryman rams "home" his bullet in preparation to fire.

UNION CAVALRY

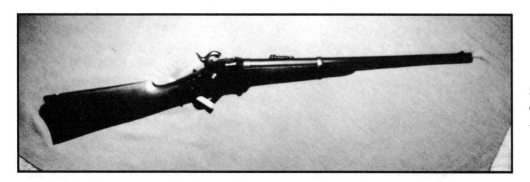

Sharps' breech-loading carbine.
Private Collection

On July 1, 1863, the Union cavalry, with only 3,500 men, held back approximately 7,600 Confederates for three hours, from 7:00 a.m. to 10:00 a.m. on McPherson Ridge west of Gettysburg. One reason the Union cavalry was able to check the advance of such an overwhelming force was because many of them carried the Sharps' breech-loading carbine.

This breech-loader was designed so that the soldier placed the entire cartridge inside a chamber next to the hammer. The breech-block was then closed, the hammer cocked, the percussion cap set in place on the nipple, and the soldier fired. Although this carbine had a shorter range than the infantry muzzle-loading rifle, it could be loaded three times faster. And in combination with more rapid fire, these carbines could be loaded and fired in a prone position, thereby giving the soldier more protection.

The Confederate cavalry was equipped with sabers, revolvers and an assortment of rifles and carbines. During and after an engagement, the Confederate cavalry attempted to confiscate discarded Union cavalry weapons because they were of a higher quality.

ARTILLERY

Throughout the Gettysburg National Military Park there are many cannon; they are primarily of three types* — one is the smoothbore, Napoleon cannon named after Napoleon III of France. The other is a rifled cannon called, a Parrott, named after its inventor, Colonel Robert P. Parrott. There are several fundamental differences between these cannon. The Napoleon was made of bronze, weighed about 1 ton and had a smoothbore. (This number includes the entire gun carriage, barrel, wheels, stock…) Due to its smoothbore design, it had a shorter range — 0-1,760 yards. The Parrott, however, was made of cast iron. The entire cannon weighed about 1,700 pounds — the barrel alone weighed 900 pounds. Within the barrel, rifling grooves increased accuracy and distance as in the infantry rifles.

"Gettysburg Gun"
12-pounder Napoleon
Range 0-1,760 yards.

During the battle a Confederate artillery shell hit directly beneath the muzzle of this cannon. Immediately following this incident, a Union artilleryman attempted to force a ball down the barrel. The ball became fixed within the damaged muzzle. The cannon was abandoned on the field essentially ready to fire.

*One will also see 3-Inch Ordnance Rifles.

Keystone Battery, Parrott 10-pounder, Range 3,520 yards.
Although not at Gettysburg, the Keystone battery is an excellent example of half a battery posing as in action.
From left to right: #1 gun loading; #2 priming; #3 firing.

The Parrott had a range of 3,520 yards (approximately two miles). Seven or eight artillerymen were needed to load and fire both these types of cannon. They were muzzle-loading, meaning, an artilleryman had to stand in front of the cannon and ram the ammunition down the barrel of the cannon. There were approximately five steps in loading the cannon. The gunner, usually a noncommissioned officer, pointed the piece and gave the command to fire. Number 1 cannoneer handled the sponge and rammer; Number 2 loaded the gun. The command, "ready," was shouted and these two men stood back from the muzzle, one on the right and the other on the left. The Number 3 man thumbed the vent with his left hand. (The vent is on the top, rear of the gun.) The Number 3 man then took a priming wire/vent pick to break open the cartridge. The Number 4 man, on the left of the breech, inserted the primer and pulled the lanyard. This ignited the powder and discharged the piece. Number 5 cannoneer then carried the ammunition from Numbers 6 or 7 at the limber chest to the Number 2 man loading the gun. A well-drilled eight-man crew was expected to fire two aimed shots per minute.[10]

Four types of ammunition were used: simple round, solid cannon balls (which looked like small bowling balls); shell; case shot, which exploded and sent pieces of shrapnel (small lead balls) and fragments through the air; and finally, canister were used at shorter ranges (usually less than 400 yards). A cannon firing canister had the effect of a large shot-gun. Between 27-96 small, round, solid balls were placed inside a canister; when the canister exited the cannon, the outer tin casing disintegrated and the small round balls were spewed out. Canister fire was capable of ripping wagon-wide holes in an on-coming infantry line.

Solid-Round Ball
MHI Collection

Case Shot
MHI Collection

Canister
MHI Collection

The Appearance of a Civil War Soldier

One also should know what the private soldier looked like, how he dressed and what equipment he carried.

For the most part Northern troops wore a dark-blue, wool blouse (jacket), sky-blue wool pants, wool socks, short ankle boots, a cotton shirt underneath the coat and under that, cotton long-underwear or drawers. The use of wool may seem illogical, especially when one remembers that the battle was in July and the temperature was at least 87°-90° coupled with extreme humidity. There were four main reasons for using wool. 1) It was heavier and more durable than other fabrics; 2) it was a tradition in the army to manufacture and issue wool clothing, and one must remember that these soldiers also campaigned during winter; 3) there was a cotton blockade affecting the shipment of cotton from the South; 4) until the Spanish American War the Quartermaster's Department refused to issue a summer or tropical weight uniform.

The Southern army was not as official in their uniforms due to several factors such as lack of funds, material, and poor transportation. The official color of the Confederate wool uniform was blue-gray; however, many soldiers wore everyday working clothes of the color "butternut" (creamy, yellow brown).

THE SOLDIER'S UNIFORM

Private William F. Chancellor, Co. A, 14th Regiment, Georgia Infantry.

Private Joseph R. Ruhl, Co. D, 150th PA (killed in action, Gettysburg)

On the march, soldiers carried between forty-five and fifty pounds of equipment (half a tent, accoutrements, blanket, food, water and ammunition); however, usually before a battle, the soldiers threw their knapsacks behind the lines and posted a few men as guards.

Though they left their burdensome paraphernalia behind, the soldiers were running and fighting in heavy clothing in the hot July weather.

One last aspect which characterized these soldiers was their ill health. Many had marched through the Pennsylvania orchard area and had been eating cherries and other fruit. In the summer heat, wearing wool clothing, marching and fighting with this condition was manifestly uncomfortable. In addition, many Civil War soldiers, because of a generally poor diet, suffered from other forms of diarrhea. This was not only bothersome but dangerous as it could cause dehydration. These illnesses and others obviously at times affected the soldiers' fighting capability.

The general appearance of a common soldier within the battle was, therefore: sweaty, lousy, foul smelling, blackened from the powder and smoke, and possibly bloody. This is not a romantic picture but a realistic one.

Strategies of the Armies

ARMY OF NORTHERN VIRGINIA
Commander, General Robert Edward Lee, age 56

In 1862, General Robert E. Lee was given command of the Army of Northern Virginia. By 1863 Lee had already gained a reputation as a fighter, gambler, and victor. In that year he out-fought four Union generals, winning major engagements: Seven Days, Virginia, June 25-July 1, 1862; Second Bull Run, August 29-30, 1862; Fredericksburg, Virginia, December 13, 1862; and, lastly, Chancellorsville, Virginia, May 1-4, 1863. The Battle of Chancellorsville was Lee's greatest victory. The morale of the Confederate Army was high, and Lee was confident that his men could achieve a great victory on Northern soil. On Friday, May 15, 1863, Lee arrived in Richmond to discuss the forthcoming campaign. Once again Lee proposed to invade the North. (His first invasion in September, 1862, ended at the Battle of Antietam, Maryland.) At this meeting five significant goals were set forth for invading Northern territory.

1) The Confederate town of Vicksburg, Mississippi, had been under siege for several weeks. If Vicksburg fell into Union hands the North would gain control of the supply line along the Mississippi — effectively splitting the Confederacy in two. By invading the North, Lee, and Confederate politicians, hoped to force Union troops to lift their siege at Vicksburg, thereby restoring Confederate control of the Mississippi River.[11]

2) Lee hoped to avoid another campaign on Virginia soil, an area already devastated by the war.

3) Due to heavy campaigning within Virginia, parts of the South were under enormous stress. Lee believed that an invasion into Northern territory would not only lure the Army of the Potomac out of the South, but more importantly, give the Southern people a brief respite from the war and "a chance to harvest their crops free from interruption by military operations."[12]

4) If the Southern army accomplished a successful campaign in the North, Jefferson Davis hoped the British Parliament would recognize the Confederacy as a separate nation and increase sorely needed economic, political and military aid.

5) Lastly, having gained a great victory at Chancellorsville, Virginia, May 1-4, 1863, Lee concluded he should follow up this success and strike the Northern army while it was still recuperating.

ARMY OF THE POTOMAC

Commander, Major General George Gordon Meade

Major General George Gordon Meade was forty-seven years old when he was informed of his new position as Commander of the Army of the Potomac. He replaced Major General Joseph Hooker. Meade was a quick, energetic soldier. Yet, one of his most distinctive characteristics was his short-temper. When he became angry he showed it. Meade was informed of his new duty on a hot Sunday morning, June 28, 1863, just three days before the battle of Gettysburg. He was quoted as saying: "Well, I've been tried and condemned without a hearing and I suppose I shall have to go to execution."[13]

Meade, who had lived in Pennsylvania prior to the war, planned a defensive strategy in accordance with the order from Washington, D.C.:

...[K]eep in view the important fact that the ARMY OF THE POTOMAC is the covering army of Washington, as well as the army of operation against the invading forces of the enemy. You will therefore manoeuvre [sic] and fight in such a manner as to cover the Capital and also Baltimore, as far as circumstances will admit. Should General Lee move upon either of these places, it is expected that you will either anticipate him or arrive with him, so as to give him battle.[14]

His first goal was to protect the capital and Baltimore, Maryland. Secondly, Meade wanted to find a solid defensive position, force Lee to attack his army, and compel the Confederates to retreat.

The Army of the Potomac was near Frederick, Maryland, and on June 29, it began marching toward Pennsylvania, screening Washington, D.C. and searching for such a defensive locale.

The Psychological Character of the Armies

THE ARMY OF NORTHERN VIRGINIA:

From the beginning of the war the Confederate army was greatly outnumbered by the Union army, but had won several major battles. In the Battle of Chancellorsville, Virginia, in May they defeated the larger Union army, but they lost one of their greatest generals—Lieutenant General Thomas "Stonewall" Jackson. During many prior campaigns Lee had given Jackson complete command of half the Confederate army, while Lee himself commanded the other half. At Gettysburg, Lee found himself having to try and oversee the entire field of battle of twenty-five square miles. He could not be everywhere at all times.

Nevertheless, the soldiers were confident in their commanders and in themselves. Lee had led them from victory to victory for over a year, and they believed this campaign would be another.[15]

THE ARMY OF THE POTOMAC:

Since the beginning of the war in 1861, the Union army had fought two draws—South Mountain, September 14, and Antietam, September 17, 1862. They had suffered many defeats. Within the past year they had lost at Fredericksburg, Virginia (December 1862) and Chancellorsville, Virginia (May 1863). Also, they had changed commanders four times. Although they continued to have confidence in their fighting ability, the men suffered under the depressing effect of several setbacks due to poor leadership. To add to their problems, two-year enlistments were expiring, and some trained veterans were going home. Consequently, many units were not at full strength.

PSYCHOLOGICAL CHARACTER OF A CIVIL WAR SOLDIER

More than ninety percent of all American Civil War soldiers were volunteers, the largest volunteer army in military history. Thousands thronged to join the Confederate and Union armies. While States Rights, strong Federal rule and issues concerning slavery were the sparks that set fire to the conflict, adventure and personal glory were the principal incentives for enlistment. Since much of the fighting occurred on Southern soil, many from the South felt that they were fighting for their own property, their farms and lands.

Those young men brought with them, too, their moral principles from home from which their actions were a direct extension. They applied their values in combat and in camp life. The great motivators for staying in the fight were personal courage, manliness, and regimental pride, to name only a few. Moreover, many of the volunteers had grown up in the same town with their comrades; therefore, their actions on and off the field were reported at home in letters and newspapers. A soldier's cowardly acts were quickly known and disgrace soon followed, not only for the individual but for his family as well. Also, by 1863, many men had campaigned together for two years, further developing a sense of loyalty toward their comrades and personal pride in their units.

In addition, as stated above, Civil War officers did not merely order their men into battle, they often led them. Seeing an officer leading a charge instilled in an individual a sense of devotion, firing his desire to follow the officer's example. While that was true most of the time, there are recorded cases where others attempted to flee inevitable danger.

Once inspired by brave leadership, one American could, indeed, kill another. When one examines Civil War soldiers' descriptions of battle, the student may be able to comprehend even this dimension to war. One veteran maintained that "a soldier on the fighting line is possessed by a demon of destruction. He wants to kill," epitomizing the kill-or-be-killed instinct.[16] Another described the fighting on the first day at Gettysburg: "[O]ur fighting blood was up and we were insensible to danger."[17]

The March to Gettysburg

ARMY OF NORTHERN VIRGINIA:

The army started its march on June 3, 1863, down the Shenandoah Valley.[18] The journey was approximately two-hundred miles, over mountains and on dirt roads and through torrential thunder storms.

On June 22, a significant incident occurred. Lee suggested to his cavalry commander, Major General Jeb Stuart, that he take three brigades and guard the right flank of Lee's lead corps—Lieutenant General Richard Ewell's 2nd Corps—and find the location of the Union army. He was to disrupt its communication lines and commandeer supplies. Lee, however, did not specify which route Stuart should take. Scouts told Stuart that he could travel through Hopewell Gap, head in a northeasterly direction, and cross the Potomac at Seneca Ford. The cavalry could then create confusion in the Union army, gather the needed supplies, cut communication lines, and meet Ewell's corps somewhere in Pennsylvania.[19]

However, since the Confederate infantry was advancing at approximately twenty miles a day and the Union was also marching quickly, Stuart found himself cut off from his army and was unable to reestablish contact with Lee to inform him of the Union position (see map 1).[20] By June 28, the Con-

Major General Jeb Stuart

federate army was stretched some seventy-two miles—from Chambersburg to York, Pennsylvania (see map 2). At that time, a Confederate spy informed Lee that the Union army had crossed the Potomac and was bearing down on him. Realizing his army was overstretched, and with the Union dangerously closing in, Lee ordered his corps to rendezvous at Gettysburg because it was easily accessible (see map 3).

ARMY OF THE POTOMAC:

On June 16/17, 1863, the Northern army began to pursue the Army of Northern Virginia, averaging twenty miles a day. By June 29 the Union command had significantly better knowledge of the location of Confederate movements.

Map 1

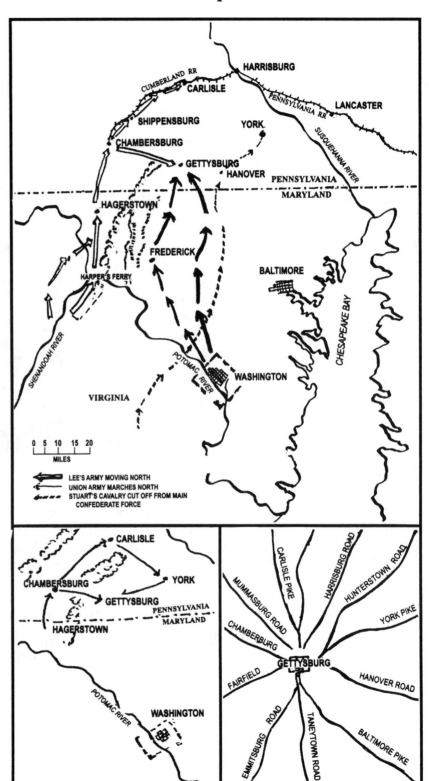

1: Note the Confederate cavalry are cut off from the main Confederate force.

2: The Confederates are spread out nearly 72 miles. Lee, therefore, orders his corps commanders to rendezvous at Gettysburg.

3: Ten roads converge at Gettysburg making it easily accessible for both armies.

Map 2

Map 3

OPPOSING COMMANDERS

MORNING JULY 1, 1863

Confederates   vs.   Union

**Third Corps Commander
Lieutenant General
Ambrose P. Hill
(22,200 men)**

**Left Wing Commander
Major General
John F. Reynolds
(11,900 men)**

**Division Commander
Major General
Henry Heth
(7,600 men)**

**First Division
Commander
Brigadier General
James Wadsworth
(3,857 men)**

**Brigade Commander
Brigadier General
James Archer
(1,048 men)**

**1st Brigade Commander
Brigadier General
Solomon Meredith
(1,800 men)**

**Brigadier General
Joseph Davis
(2,600 men)**

**2nd Brigade Commander
Brigadier General
Lysander Cutler
(1,600 men)**

Union Cavalry Commanders

**First Division
Brigadier General
John Buford
(2,748 men)**

**1st Brigade
Colonel William
Gamble
(1,600 men)**

**2nd Brigade
Colonel Thomas
Devin
(1,148 men)**

Tour I

Stop 1: McPherson's Ridge
(Gettysburg National Park Stop 1)

THE PRELUDE

Time: **Tuesday, June 30, 1863**
Setting: **Just west of Gettysburg on the Chambersburg and Mummasburg Roads.**

ARMY OF NORTHERN VIRGINIA:

A Confederate brigade (2,400 infantry from Heth's division) approached Gettysburg from the west.[21] On reaching the suburbs, the brigade found Union cavalry in the town. The officers believed that they were supported by infantry. A captain reported the Union force was, indeed, well-trained and probably part of the army. Yet, his commanders assumed they were only local, unprofessional militia. Heth, commander of the lead division, asked his corps commander, Lieutenant General Ambrose P. Hill, if he could take his men (7,600) into Gettysburg—Wednesday, July 1—to obtain needed supplies, especially shoes. Hill voiced no objection.[22]

Because there were no shoes at Gettysburg on July 1, Heth's primary intention may have been to force an encounter. Four days earlier Confederate Major General Jubal Early's division swept through the town and commandeered most of the supplies, including the much needed shoes.

ARMY OF THE POTOMAC:

The Union cavalry commander, Brigadier General John Buford, reported at 10:40 p.m., June 30, that Hill's Confederate corps (22,200 men) was massed near Cashtown approximately nine miles west of Gettysburg.[23] Because of its easy access the town was in a strategic location. These roads led to Washington D.C., Baltimore, Harrisburg (capital of Pennsylvania) and many more cities. The Union infantry vanguard was ordered to occupy Gettysburg.[24] On the night of June 30, however, the leading infantry corps was about five miles south of Gettysburg. It was therefore left to the cavalry to hold the town and delay the imposing numbers of Confederates until the Union infantry could arrive.

Buford realized his task was difficult. His division numbered only 2,748 men, and the Confederates numbered at least twice that many (7,600). Buford, however, used the excellent defensive positions in and around the town. Recognizing that mounted charges into infantry were suicidal, Buford also employed a tactic which made it possible for his small division to hold the Confederates for three hours; he treated his cavalry as mounted infantry and used them as foot-soldiers.

THE BATTLE

Time: Wednesday Morning, July 1, 1863.
First Stage: 7:30 a.m.-10:00 a.m.
Setting: Three miles west of Gettysburg on the Chambersburg Pike near Herr Ridge and Whisler's Ridge, Union position.

Buford ordered his cavalry to dismount and fight on foot. Using trees, fences or lying prone for cover, his men could delay the Confederate infantry until the rest of the Union forces arrived. Because they were dismounted, one man in every four was required to hold the horses behind the J. Herbst's Woods (also known as McPherson's Woods).

Near Marsh Creek, at approximately 7:30 a.m., the Union pickets spotted the Confederate vanguard. Lieutenant Marcellus Jones of the 8th Illinois Cavalry fired a shot at a Confederate officer, but he could not see whether he hit his target.

It was not until 8:00 a.m. that the Confederates advanced. The Union pickets retreated and formed a new battle line east of Willoughby Run. From the Lutheran Seminary cupola, on Seminary Ridge, Buford saw the enemy advancing. He then ordered Colonel William Gamble, with 1,600 troops, to join the pickets along Willoughby Run. The cavalry was stretched in a thin line—from the Fairfield Road to an unfinished railroad bed north of the Chambersburg turnpike. On the northern side of the railroad cut to Oak Hill, several units from Colonel Thomas Devin's brigade were deployed. In addition, Devin had squadrons watching the roads north of the town in order to stall the Confederate troops who were coming from the Carlisle-York area (see map 4). For one hour Buford's troopers, who were well protected by a stone wall and armed with breech-loading carbines (which could be loaded three times as fast as an infantry muzzle-loading rifle), detained two brigades (those of Brigadier General James Archer and Brigadier General Joseph Davis) until 9:00 a.m. By that time, however, the cavalry had fallen back to a new position on McPherson's Ridge, which was approximately 200 yards from the first line (see map 5).

Major General John F. Reynolds, commander of the left wing, joined Buford at the Seminary. Ar-

Post-war photo:
Lieutenant Marcellus Jones

riving ahead of his infantry, Reynolds asked Buford if his troops could hold a little longer. Buford replied, "I reckon I can." For the next hour and forty-five minutes, 9:00-10:45 a.m., the cavalrymen on McPherson's Ridge checked the Confederate advance. At approximately 10:45 a.m. the two leading Union infantry brigades arrived, and the second stage of the July 1st battle commenced.

There were several reasons for the cavalry's successful defense of the town: 1) a strong, natural defensive position for the first and second battle lines; 2) the faster rate of fire of the carbine with which they were armed; 3) ignorant of the numbers of the opposition and whether they were militia or trained veteran soldiers, Confederate General Heth moved with caution against Gettysburg, sending in only two of his four brigades.

Map 4 — McPherson's Ridge

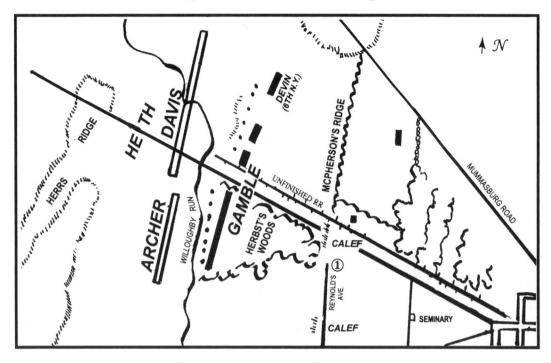

July 1, 8:00 a.m., near Willoughby Run.
Two Confederate brigades attacked Buford's cavalrymen.

Map 5 — McPherson's Ridge

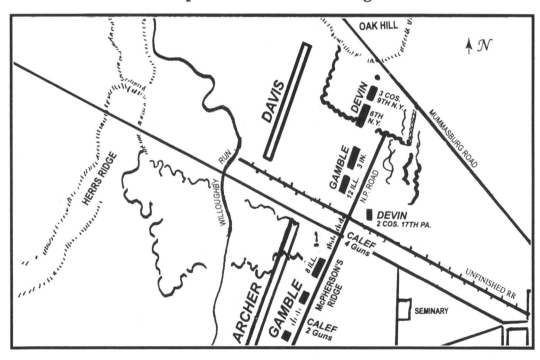

July 1, 9:00 a.m.
Buford's cavalrymen fall back to McPherson's Ridge.

Second Stage: 10:45-11:00 a.m.

Having marched nearly eight miles, the vanguard of the Union Ist Corps double-quicked the last one-and-a-half miles across the fields. Furthermore, while they were running, they were ordered to load their rifles.

Brigadier General Lysander Cutler's brigade was the first to arrive. Reynolds placed two regiments south of the Chambersburg Pike with six cannon to their immediate right. The remainder of the brigade was lined to the right of the un-finished railroad bed.

Immediately following Cutler's brigade was the famous "Iron Brigade," commanded by Brigadier General Solomon Meredith, known for their steady fighting ability and their dis-tinctive black hats.

The Iron Brigade's position was on the south side of the Chambersburg Pike — left of Cutler's brigade (see map 6).

Note the black-hat style of the Iron Brigade.

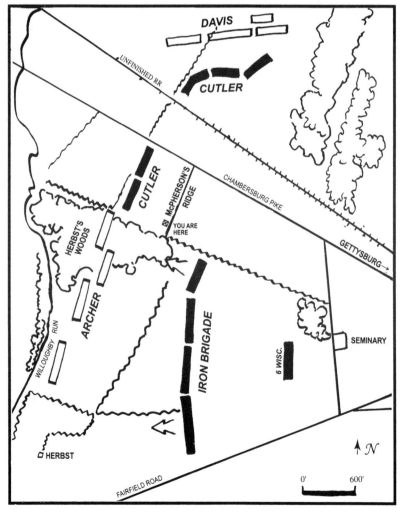

Map 6 — McPherson's Ridge
Meredith's "Iron Brigade" and
Cutler's brigade.

Second Stage: Archer's Brigade   vs.   Meredith's "Iron Brigade"
                          (1,048)   (1,800)

As the Union cavalry fell back through their infantry, an 8th Illinois cavalryman refused to yield his ground. As the enemy drew near, he stood and shouted, "Come on — We have them!" The Rebels were startled; they did not see anyone behind the soldier. A moment later, however, the leading regiment of the Iron Brigade smashed into the Confederates and the other regiments followed.[25] The blow was like a sledge hammer continuously striking at the target.

At that moment Reynolds, who was on his horse directing the Union troops into the woods, was shot through the head and killed.

Two Iron Brigade regiments were ordered to swing right, around the woods, to strike at the Confederate rear. When the troops attacked, a Rebel stated, "Here are those damned black-hat fellers again ... Tain't no militia—that's the Army of the Potomac!" (see map 7).[26]

Having successfully outflanked and nearly surrounded Archer's Brigade, the Iron Brigade captured a large number of Confederates, including Archer himself.[27] The remaining troops escaped to Herr Ridge.

Go to Stop 2:
John Burns' Statue.

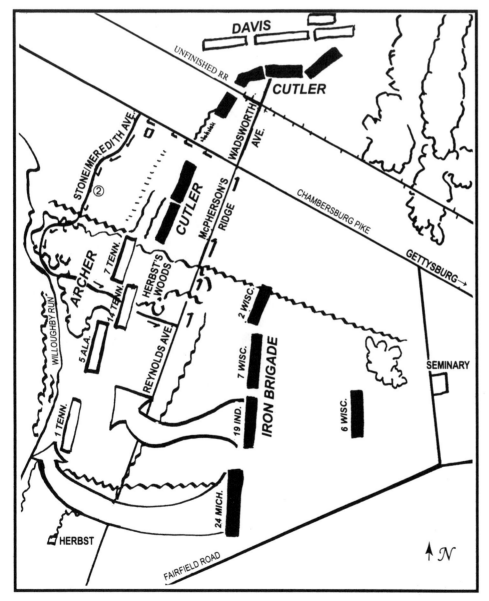

Map 7
McPherson's Ridge
24th Michigan and 19th Indiana flank Archer's brigade.

Stop 2: John Burns Monument

VIGNETTE ON JOHN BURNS

John Burns was a sixty-nine year old resident of Gettysburg. On the first day of battle he went out to Herbst's Woods to aid the Union troops and to fight alongside the 150th Pennsylvania. He was wounded several times but survived his injuries. Nine years later, 1872, he died at the age of seventy-eight.

John Burns

Go to Stop 3: The Railroad Cut

Stop 3: The Railroad Cut/Wadsworth Avenue

THE UNFINISHED RAILROAD CUT

Second Stage: 10:45-11:00 a.m.

While the Union troops were severely punishing the Confederates in Herbst's Woods, Cutler's brigade—on the right—was being outflanked by the overwhelming force of Confederates. Under pressure, he ordered his three regiments (right of the railroad bed) to fall back. Two of his regiments retreated to the next wooded ridge (Seminary Ridge). In the midst of the confusion, one regiment (147th New York) did not retreat. The Confederates were in possession of the railroad cut, and were threatening to surround the New York regiment. To avoid total annihilation an officer ordered his men to retreat to Seminary Ridge (see map 8). During the half-hour which elapsed before the regiment withdrew, the 147th New York suffered 207 killed and wounded out of 380.[28]

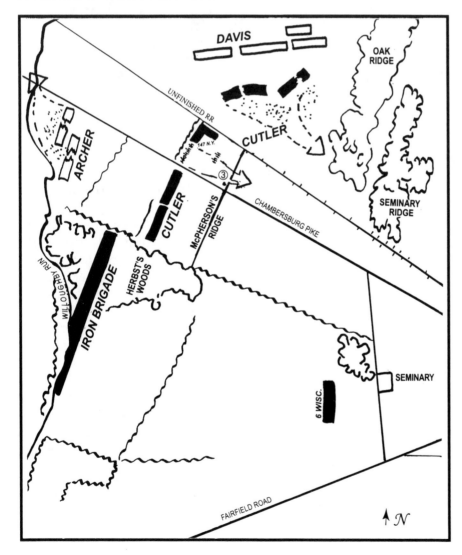

Map 8 — Railroad Cut
Cutler's brigade is forced back to Seminary Ridge; the 147th NY is isolated, and the Iron brigade's right flank is threatened

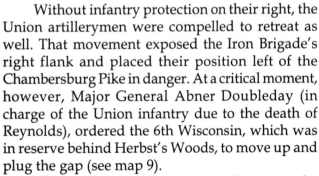

Major General Abner Doubleday
(Shown here in his Brigidier General's Uniform.)

Lieutenant Colonel Rufus Dawes

Without infantry protection on their right, the Union artillerymen were compelled to retreat as well. That movement exposed the Iron Brigade's right flank and placed their position left of the Chambersburg Pike in danger. At a critical moment, however, Major General Abner Doubleday (in charge of the Union infantry due to the death of Reynolds), ordered the 6th Wisconsin, which was in reserve behind Herbst's Woods, to move up and plug the gap (see map 9).

Having received his orders to "move to the right" and "go like hell,"[29] Lieutenant Colonel Rufus Dawes, of the 6th Wisconsin, charged with his 420 soldiers. When they reached a fence parallel to the Chambersburg Pike, Dawes ordered his men to fire into the right flank of Davis's brigade. Joining the 6th Wisconsin were two regiments of Cutler's brigade, the 95th and 84th New York, which were earlier deployed on the left side of the Chambersburg Pike. Their fire forced the Confederates into the railroad bed, where they regrouped to meet the attack. The railroad cut functioned as a convenient trench for a while. Dawes then commanded his regiment over the fence, making them vulnerable to Confederate fire. Encouraging his troops Dawes shouted, "Align on the colors! Close up on the colors! Close up on the colors!"[30] Upon reaching the railroad embankment, seventy-five yards from the fence, they engaged the 2nd Mississippi and 55th North Carolina. A Wisconsin private grabbed for the Confederate flag but was shot down. Another Wisconsin trooper then wielded his rifle like a club and brained the Confederate who had shot his friend. The flag was captured and the Confederates found themselves trapped within the trench, the sides of which rise up to twenty feet in places. All along the embankment the Union troops pointed their rifles into the channel and shouted, "Throw down your muskets! Throw down your muskets!"[31]

The Union battle line was thus saved in this sector. For two hours a quiet respite fell upon the field.

In this charge, which covered approximately 175 yards, out of the 420 men, 160 Wisconsin soldiers were either killed or wounded.[32]

Map 9 — The Railroad Cut

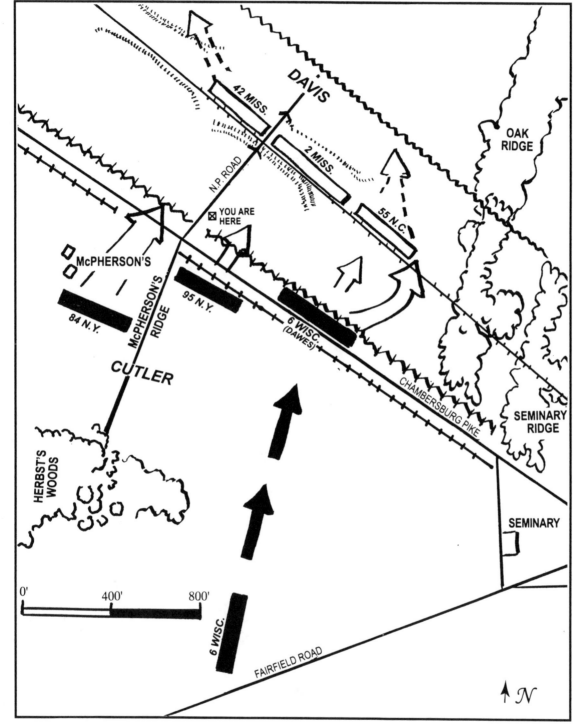

The 6th Wisconsin sprints, by column, across the field (behind McPherson's Ridge) then deploys at the Chambersburg Pike, and is aided by the 84th & 95th N.Y. in the attack on Davis's brigade.

Go to Stop 4: Oak Ridge, on Doubleday Avenue.

July 1 — Respite 11:00 a.m.-2:00 p.m.

Still unaware of the Union strength, Davis's and Archer's brigades pulled back to Herr Ridge in order to regroup. Lee arrived on the battlefield in the early afternoon. At the same time, Confederate Major General Robert Rodes arrived with his division (8,600 men) and deployed his troops on the left flank of Heth's division.

On the Union side, the remaining units of the I Corps (9,403 men) took position along McPherson's Ridge, Seminary Ridge, and Oak Ridge. Around 1:00 p.m. about 6,000 Union troops, from the XI Corps, deployed on the right side of Mummasburg road to the Harrisburg road. Their battle line, however, was stretched thin (see map 10).

Both sides had marched approximately ten to thirteen miles in the hot sun.

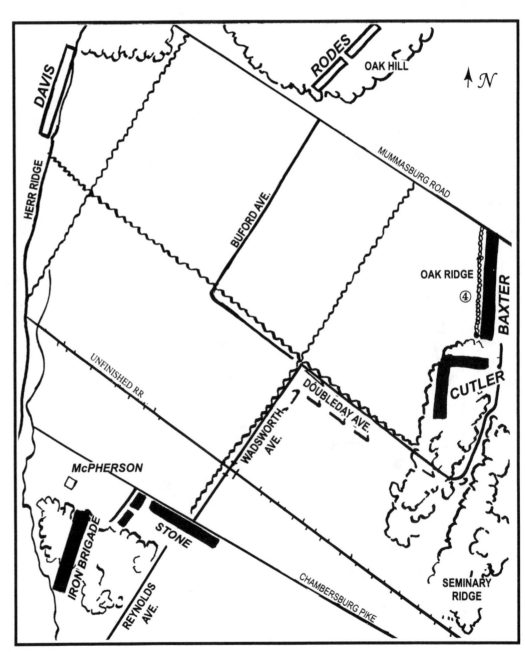

Map 10
Opposing Positions
July 1, 11:00-2:30 p.m.

Stop 4: Oak Ridge, near the stone wall on Doubleday Avenue.
(Gettysburg National Park Stop 3)

THE CONTEST ON THE UNION RIGHT FLANK.*

Second Corps Commander   vs.   **Eleventh Corps Commander**

Lieutenant General Richard Ewell
(15,900 men)+

Major General Oliver Howard
(6,000 men)**

---

* To avoid diverting the reader too far from the National Auto Tour, the fight on the Union right flank will be briefly discussed on Seminary Ridge.

\+ The 15,900 were the troops Ewell had on hand at the time. One of his divisions had not arrived yet. The total strength of his Corps was 22,200.

** General Howard actually had 10,300 in his Corps; however, he had placed 3,200 of his troops on Cemetery Hill to act as reserves. Therefore, only about 6,000 Union troops were on the right flank to meet Ewell's Confederate force. Howard was primarily in command of all the Union troops at this time on the battlefield.

THE MID-AFTERNOON BATTLE BEGINS

1:30-3:30 p.m.

Confederate Division Commander: vs.   **Union Division Commander:**

Major General Robert Rodes
(8,600 men)

Brigadier General John C. Robinson*
(4,100 men)

Brigade Commanders: vs.   **Brigade Commander:**

Colonel Edward A. O'Neal
(1,688 men)

Brigadier General Henry Baxter
(1,200 men)

Brigade Commander:
Brigadier General Alfred Iverson
(1,450 men)

*Brigadier General Gabriel Paul also helped repulse Iverson's brigade.

INITIAL ENCOUNTER ON OAK RIDGE AND FORNEY'S FIELD

Between 1:30-2:00 p.m.[33]

Rodes placed approximately sixteen cannon on Oak Hill. The cannon sent a deadly fire across the Union line to the Fairfield road. Rodes planned that Colonel Edward A. O'Neal's brigade, stationed on the other side of the ridge, would move obliquely to Oak Ridge (see map 11). Brigadier General Alfred Iverson was to send his brigade across the field and hit the Union line on Seminary Ridge at an angle. Attacking at an oblique angle would allow O'Neal's and Iverson's brigades to concentrate on the Union right flank, thereby throwing it into disorder.

On the Union side, Brigadier General Henry Baxter deployed part of his brigade behind the stone wall which paralleled the Mummasburg Road. The rest of the brigade was behind the stone wall on Doubleday's Avenue. Seeing O'Neal's brigade, the Union troops facing north-west fired into them. Also, posted at right angles to Baxter's brigade, facing west, was part of the Third Division of the 11th Corps (refer to map 11).

Between 1:30 and 2:00 p.m., O'Neal's brigade attacked; however, due to battle confusion, only three of the four regiments assaulted the Union right flank. Iverson failed to attack with O'Neal's brigade.

The charge was doomed from the start. Attacking on a narrow front, on the eastern side of Oak Hill and Ridge, the Confederate brigade was caught in a deadly cross fire, the Union 3rd Division firing into their left flank, while their front met a storm of rifle fire from Baxter's brigade. O'Neal's brigade was quickly beaten back with great loss; 512 Confederates were killed or wounded out of 1,688.

Go to Stop 5:
Forney's Field, Buford Avenue.

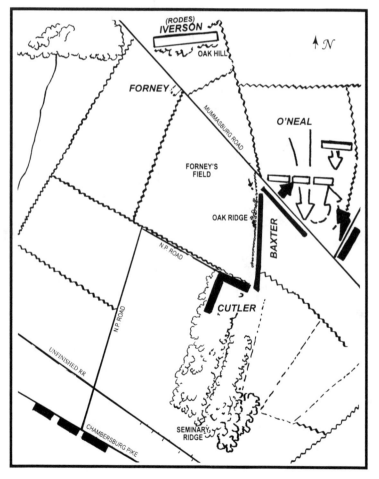

Map 11
Oak Ridge
Colonel O'Neal's brigade is repulsed.
Nearly 500 Alabama troops are killed or wounded.

Stop 5: Forney's Field, Buford Avenue

THE INITIAL CONTEST IN FORNEY'S FIELD

Second Stage

Back on Oak Hill, Iverson delayed his assault so that the Confederate cannon could effectively clear Oak and Seminary Ridge. But O'Neal's brigade had attacked, leaving Iverson's left flank unprotected. In addition, it gave Baxter's Union brigade time to change front again, so that his men now faced west, hidden behind the stone wall. Behind them was a slope. Consequently, the Confederate brigade could not see the Union soldiers and, unknowingly, the North Carolina soldiers marched into a deathtrap (see map 12).

Ordering his brigade forward, Iverson stayed behind on Oak Hill to watch the assault. The Confederates advanced southeast toward the Union line on Seminary Ridge. As they crossed the field their left flank began to drift towards the stone wall on Oak Ridge. When they were only 80 yards from the stone wall, the Union soldiers rose up and sent a destructive volley of fire into Iverson's brigade.

Approximately 455 of them fell, either killed or wounded, "in a line as straight as a dress parade."[34] Worse yet, Cutler's Union brigade swung around from the west to the north and poured in a deadly cross-fire, and another regiment on the Chambersburg Pike, facing north, fired into their right flank as well (see map 12). A soldier from the 23rd North Carolina described the blood bath.

...[T]he enemy rose from its protected lair and poured into us a withering fire from the front and both flanks...Pressing forward with heavy loss under deadly fire our regiment, which was the second from the right, reached a hollow or low place...Unable to advance, unwilling to retreat, the brigade layed down in this hollow... and fought as best it could...Major C. C. Blacknall was shot through the mouth and neck...Lieutenant-Colonel R. D. Johnson...and Colonel D. H. Christie were mortally wounded,

Major C. C. Blacknall survived his wounds.

Lieutenant Colonel R. D. Johnson

Colonel D. H. Christie

as the line lay in the bloody hollow...A member of the Twenty-Third layed stone dead, his musket clinched in his hand and five bullets through his head...[35]

One of Baxter's regiments charged the horribly devasted Confederates and captured hundreds of North Carolinians. In addition to the 455 men killed and wounded in Iverson's brigade 308 were captured or missing, a total of 763 out of 1,450. Over half the brigade had been wiped out.

The 23rd North Carolina casualty rate was: 136 either killed or wounded out of 372 soldiers, over a third.

Go to Stop 6: Lutheran Seminary, Seminary Avenue.

Map 12

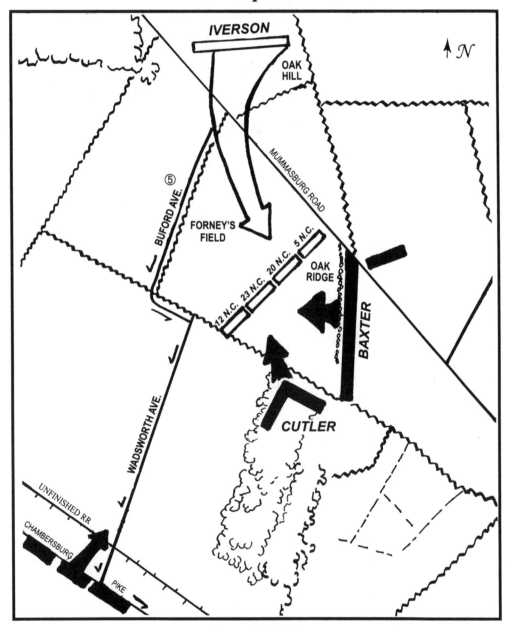

Forney's Field
Iverson's brigade attacks and is caught in a cross-fire.
Approximately 500 North Carolinians are killed or wounded in this field.

Stop 6: Lutheran Seminary, Seminary Avenue

THE FINAL PUSH: THE UNION ARMY FORCED TO RETREAT

At roughly 3:00 p.m. twelve Confederate cannon on the Harrisburg road sent a sweeping fire along the length of the Union right flank (in military terms this is called an enfilading fire). Then, appearing out near the road, Confederate Major General Jubal Early's division (6,300 men) charged the extreme right of the Union 11th Corps and outflanked their position. The Union soldiers defended their battle line for a brief time but were soon compelled to retreat through the town (see map 13).

With the XI Corps in full retreat, the Union I Corps, back on Oak Ridge and Seminary Ridge, were soon forced to retire. They slowly and stubbornly withdrew from McPherson's Ridge and Seminary Ridge to the area around Cemetery Hill.

Major General Jubal Early

Map 13

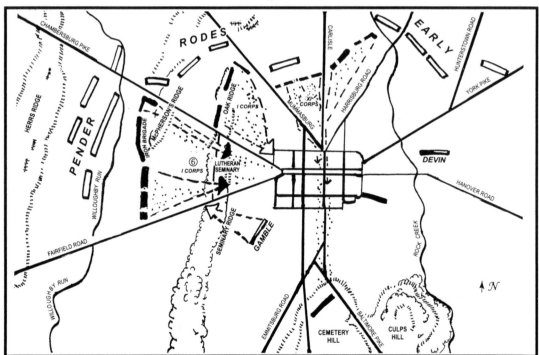

Seminary Avenue
July 1, 3:30-4:00 p.m.

The Union right flank (XI Corps) falls back through Gettysburg. The Union I Corps, on the left flank, slowly gives way.

THE FINAL CONFEDERATE PUSH ON THE UNION LEFT FLANK

Confederate Corps Commander: vs.   **Union Corps Commander:**

Lieutenant General Ambrose P. Hill   *Major General Abner Doubleday

Division Commander: vs.   **Division Commander:**

Major General William Pender+   Brigadier General James Wadsworth
(6,735 men)   (3,857 men)**

*   After Reynolds was killed, Doubleday took command of the I Corps.

\+   Major General William Pender was wounded in the leg on July 2, 1863. He later died from this wound.

** Meredith's Iron Brigade and Cutler's brigade made up the division. Their total strength was lower at that time, having already been engaged in battle.

Colonel Samuel Williams

Colonel Henry Morrow

While the Union right flank was being struck, Hill renewed his attack on the Union left (approximately 3:00 p.m.). After an almost relentless struggle, the Iron Brigade was forced out of J. Herbst's Woods back to Seminary Ridge. There the Union artillerymen waited until the Confederate line was 100 yards away and fired double charges of canister into their lines. They staggered but soon continued their attack. Colonel Samuel Williams of the 19th Indiana (part of the Iron Brigade) shouted, "We must hold the colors on this line, or lie here under them."[36] To the right of the 19th Indiana, Colonel Henry Morrow of the 24th Michigan, rallied the men of Wayne County. But the Iron Brigade was forced off of Seminary Ridge. It formed another battle line, behind a fence, just east of the Ridge (see map 14).

Map 14

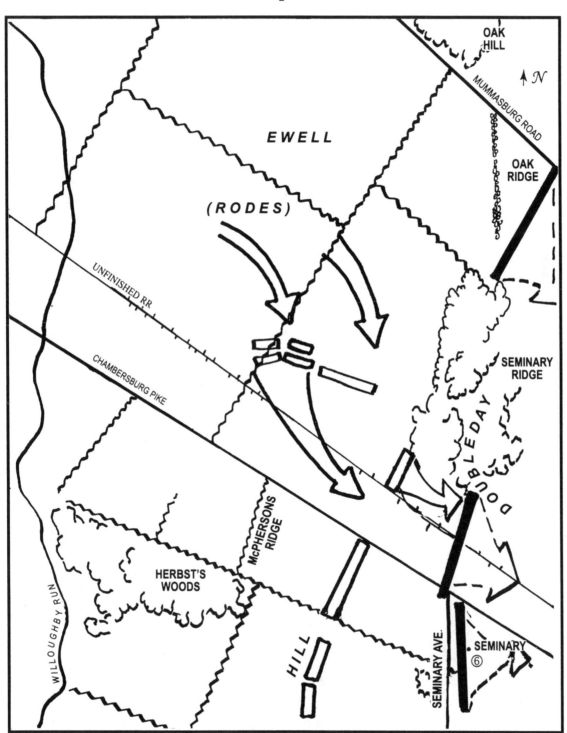

The Union left flank retreats.

Finally, after six separate battle lines had been formed between Herbst's Woods and the east side of Seminary Ridge, around 3:45 p.m. the Iron Brigade (Union I Corps) was ordered to fall back to Cemetery Hill. To protect the retreating infantry, Colonel William Gamble and his dismounted cavalry were ordered to cover their retreat. They deployed behind the fence and sent a "perfectly terrific" fire into the Confederates. Tired, hot and needing reinforcements, the Confederates stopped on Seminary Ridge (see map 15).[37]

* * * *

Map 15

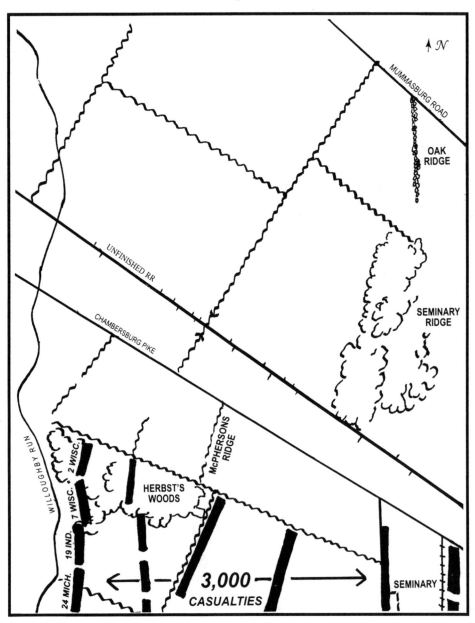

Seminary Ridge
July 1, 10:45-4:30 p.m.
The Iron Brigade forms six seperate battles lines.

Hill discontinued his attack on the Federal troops for several reasons:[38] 1) He was under the impression that the Union soldiers were entirely disorganized and routed; 2) his men had been fighting hard for six hours and were near exhaustion; 3) due to the intensity of combat, the Confederates had sustained heavy casualties and were disorganized themselves.

Cemetery Hill rises 80 feet above Gettysburg and Culp's Hill about 100 feet. Whoever controlled these heights could virtually command the surrounding area. Lee, recognizing the topographical importance of Cemetery Hill and Culp's Hill, sent a message to Lieutenant General Richard Ewell asking him to seize the high ground if Ewell thought it possible. Ewell's corps was situated on the north side of Gettysburg. He, however, believed that at that time—between 4:30-5:30 p.m.—his troops could not take the heights. His reasons were: 1) he could not effectively bombard Cemetery Hill because he was unable to position his artillery in an advantageous site; 2) one of his divisions had not arrived at Gettysburg and the only troops at his disposal were "jaded by twelve hours' marching and fighting;"[39] 3) his men were also disorganized due to driving the enemy soldiers through the narrow streets and alleys of the town; 4) nearly 4,000 Union troops had been captured, which meant Ewell had to detail several hundred of his men to guard them.

Moreover, this was the first major battle in which Ewell directly served under Lee. Always before Ewell had answered to Lieutenant General Jackson whose orders were more direct and left little decision-making up to him.[40]

* * * *

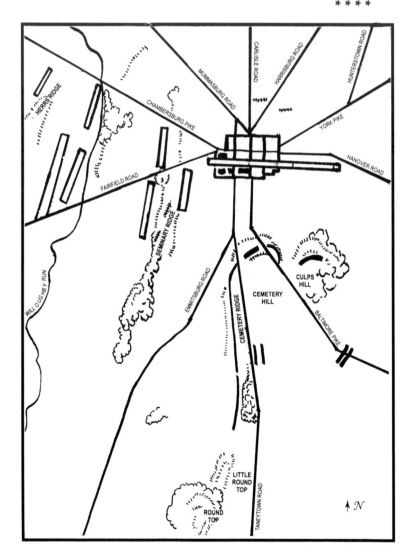

Around 5:00 p.m., on Cemetery Hill, about 12,000 Union soldiers built fortifications around Cemetery Hill and Ridge. At 6:00 p.m. their reinforcements arrived. The Union strength was now about 20,000 and their defenses secure (see map 16).

Map 16
Seminary Ridge
July 1, midnight-July 2, 8:00-11:00 a.m.
Confederate and Union positions.

SUMMARY OF WEDNESDAY, JULY 1, 1863

General Lee ordered his corps commanders to rendezvous near Gettysburg. Yet he did not expect to fight at this small town. On the morning of July 1 a Confederate division, commanded by Major General Henry Heth, made a forced reconnaissance into Gettysburg. They were, however, detained by Brigadier General John Buford's cavalry. For three hours the dismounted horsemen checked the infantrymen. Finally, the Confederates made a forced assault and pushed the cavalry from their position. At this time (between 10:30-10:45 a.m.) Major General John Reynolds arrived at Gettysburg with two Union brigades. Recognizing the strong defensive position in and around the town, Reynolds determined to stand and fight there. Shortly after his arrival on the field, while directing the Iron Brigade into battle, he was shot and killed. For five-and-a-half, hard-fought hours the two sides battled (10:30-4:00 p.m.). By 4:00 p.m. the two Union corps (I and XI) were overwhelmed by sheer numbers. They retreated back through the town and established a strong defensive position on Culp's Hill, Cemetery Hill and Cemetery Ridge. Exhausted and disorganized by the day's fighting, the Confederates broke off their attack.

Casualties: The casualty list for July 1 was extremely high. In the area between J. Herbst's Woods and the fence east of Seminary Ridge, where the Iron Brigade fought, at least 3,000 Union and Confederate soldiers were either killed or wounded (see map 15). A Confederate Captain, crossing this area after the battle, heard the "dreadful—not moans but howls—of some of the wounded. It was so distressing that . . . [he] approached several with the purpose of calming them if possible. [He] . . . found them foaming at the mouth as if mad."[41]

The Iron Brigade suffered nearly 886 killed and wounded and 266 were missing, a total of 1,152 out of 1,800 engaged; only 648 remained. The 19th Indiana lost 210 killed, wounded, and missing, out of 308. Ninety-eight men answered roll-call the next day. The 24th Michigan lost 277 of their 496 men, either killed or wounded, and 86 were captured or missing—leaving 133 survivors.[42]

The 26th North Carolina Regiment, which clashed primarily with the 24th Michigan, sustained even worse casualties. In about two hours' fighting the 800 North Carolinians engaged suffered 588 killed or wounded; 212 remained.

Overall Union soldiers killed and wounded on this day were at least 5,960. The Confederates lost 7,432 men, a total of 13,392 in only five-and-a-half hours of fighting.[43]

LEE AND HIS GENERALS TAKE THE INITIATIVE

**Evening of July 1 and Thursday Morning, 2 July
5:00 p.m.-3:00 a.m.**

As the fighting subsided on July 1, Lee and Lieutenant General James Longstreet considered the situation. As the commander of the Confederate First Corps, Longstreet was Lee's chief lieutenant. Through field glasses, they studied the Union position on Culp's Hill and Cemetery Hill/Ridge. Longstreet concluded that the Union line was too strong at that point, and he advised Lee not to attack at Gettysburg. Instead, he suggested that they make a sweeping movement southward along their own right, then veer toward the east to move around the left of Meade's army. Characteristically, Longstreet preferred to locate a strong defensive position and make the enemy come to him. Lee, however, stated that if the Union army remained in Gettysburg on July 2nd, he would attack.

Lee based his strategy on information that the Union line extended along Culp's Hill, Cemetry Hill and Ridge (the line stopping where the Pennsylvania Monument now stands). He proposed a three-pronged attack upon their position.

1) Longstreet was ordered to place his troops secretly on the right flank and command the main thrust of the attack. His orders were to attack up the Emmitsburg road, roll up their left flank and hit Cemetery Hill.

2) Hill's men, coming from the west, were to hit the Union center on Cemetery Ridge and Cemetery Hill and seek to prevent reinforcements being sent to either flank (see map 17).

3) Ewell's corps, on the Confederate left flank, would make a "simultaneous demonstration upon the enemy's right [near Culp's Hill and east-Cemetery Hill] to be converted into a real attack should opportunity offer."[44]

Lee had approximately 50,000 troops and 200 cannon at his disposal.

MEADE DEPLOYS THE UNION ARMY

Thursday, 2 July
1:00 a.m.-3:00 p.m.

Meade reached Gettysburg around 1:00 a.m. on July 2nd. Informed that Lee was concentrating his army at Gettysburg, Meade determined to stand and fight. Throughout the morning, he reconnoitered the areas of Cemetery Hill, Cemetery Ridge and Culp's Hill. As his army arrived piecemeal, Meade stationed troops on Culp's Hill, Cemetery Hill and Ridge. A strong defensive position was established, for several reasons: 1) Two subordinate generals had expressed their disapproval of taking the offensive; 2) One corps still had not arrived; 3) Meade realized his men were worn out from intense marching and might not be able to sustain the strain of an offensive assault. 4) Lastly, he recognized the high ground as a natural defensive position which would provide the advantage.[45] By 3:00 p.m. the entire Army of the Potomac was massed around Gettysburg. At least 70,000 soldiers and over 350 cannon were at Meade's disposal [46]* and were deployed in strategic locations (see map 17).

*Figures arrived at by taking into consideration the Federal losses of July 1.

Go to Stop 7:
North Carolina Monument,
West Confederate Avenue

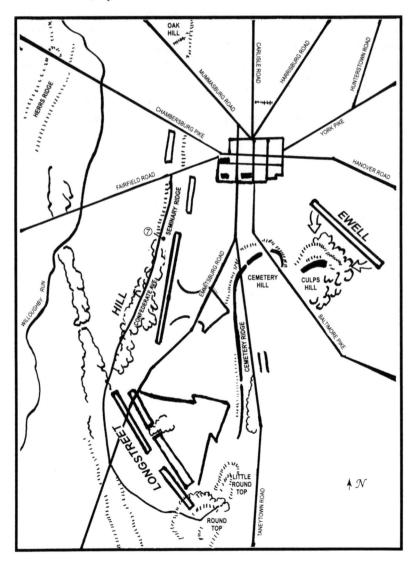

Map 17
July 2
Lee's proposed three-pronged attack.

Stop 7: North Carolina Monument, West Confederate Avenue
(Gettysburg National Park Stop 4)

THE UNION LINE FROM THE CONFEDERATE VIEW

July 2nd and 3rd

From here Lee could see two-thirds of the Union line. To the far right is a rocky hill (Little Round Top) and a larger, wooded hill (Big Round Top). Little Round Top was significant because it was the highest, cleared ground commanding this area. Whoever controlled this ground could position cannon which would command Cemetery Ridge and Cemetery Hill. Consequently, on July 2, the region around Little Round Top was the scene of a bloody two-and-a-half hours of fighting. Ahead is Cemetery Ridge and Hill. At the center of the ridge is a small copse of trees toward which Lee instructed his generals to advance on July 3rd.

The assault on the 3rd day was christened "Pickett's Charge," primarily because Major General George Pickett was the commander of a full division, and his division suffered the heaviest casualties (see map 18).[47]

The details of this charge will be discussed on Cemetery Ridge—Stops 23a-e.

Go to Stop 8: Virginia Monument, West Confederate Avenue

Map 18

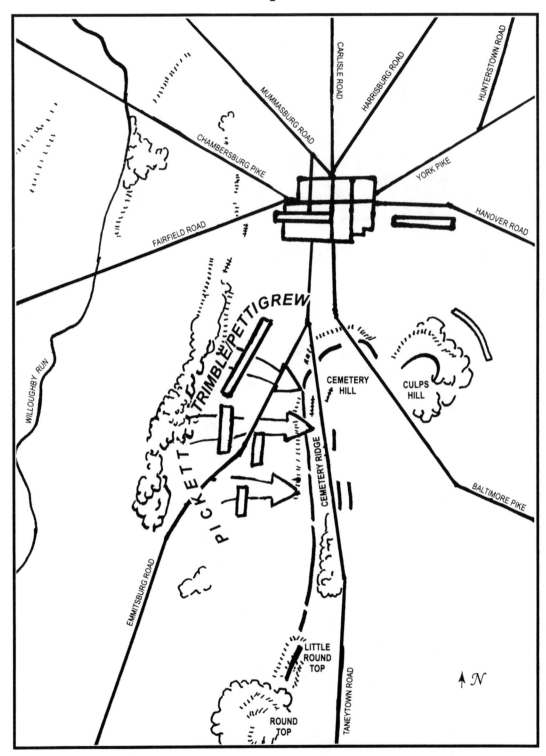

July 3, 3:00-4:00 p.m.
"Pickett's, Pettigrew's and Trimble's Charge."
An overview of the final asault on Cemetery Ridge.

Stop 8: General Robert E. Lee and the Virginia Monument
(Gettysburg National Park Stop 5)

From here Lee watched the attack on Cemetery Ridge, Friday July 3, 1863. He took full responsibility for the failed attack. A Virginia officer overheard him lament, "It's all my fault! I thought my men were invincible."[48]

Go to Stop 9: Warfield Ridge, Tower, Confederate Avenue.

Stop 9: Warfield Ridge, Tower
(Gettysburg National Park Stop 7)

OPPOSING CORP COMMANDERS ON THE UNION LEFT FLANK

Thursday, July 2, 12:00-3:00 p.m.

First Confederate Corps Commander　　　vs.　　　**3rd Union Corps Commander**

Lieutenant General James Longstsreet
(15,000 men)

Major General Daniel Sickles
(10,000-12,000 men)

To concentrate the main attack on the Union left flank (his right flank), Longstreet deployed two of his divisions (nearly 15,000 men) along Warfield Ridge. They had been awakened for duty between 3:00 a.m. and 4:30 a.m. and marched from the direction of Chambersburg. They arrived near Gettysburg around 8:30 a.m. One of these brigades marched 24 miles and arrived much later in the day, about 2:00 p.m.[49] They were not only exhausted but hungry because not all the supply wagons had reached Gettysburg.

By 12:00 noon Longstreet's men, with the exception of the late arrivals, were back on the road making their way toward the left flank of the Union army. To conceal that march from the Union signal station on Little Round Top, they traveled along a small country road located behind Seminary Ridge. Their movement was nevertheless detected by the signalmen atop the hill. Not realizing that their position had been located, Longstreet, consistent with his plan to hide their approach, ordered a counter-march and proceeded on another trail. Finally, after three hours of tedious and tiresome wandering and an extra three or four miles of trudging in the dust in 85° humid weather, Longstreet's men deployed on Warfield Ridge. By the time they were prepared to attack, however, the Union battle line had been altered (see map 19).

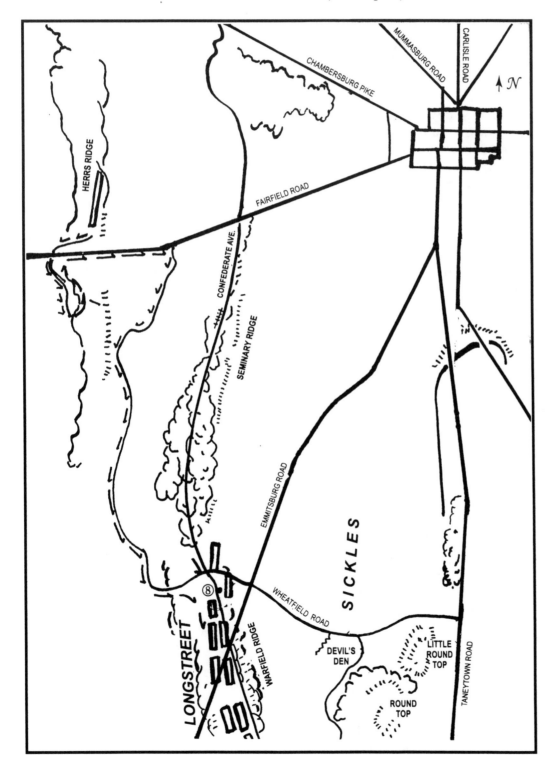

Map 19
The arrows indicate Longstreet's counter-march prior to his attack on Little Round Top/Devil's Den area.

MAJOR GENERAL DANIEL SICKLES REDEPLOYS HIS CORPS

Thursday, July 2, 2:00-3:30 p.m.

Realizing that the III Corps had been assigned to a low lying area, about 2:00 Sickles, on his own initiative, began moving between 10,000 and 12,000 men approximately half-a-mile from Cemetery Ridge to the Peach Orchard/Devil's Den area (see map 20).

He did this for several reasons. 1) He observed the higher ground in front of him—the Peach Orchard and Devil's Den area—and ascertained that if the enemy obtained this ground they could wreak havoc on his present position on Cemetery Ridge; 2) He had sent scouts out to locate the Confederates; they had reported that the Rebels were indeed in the wooded area, about a mile in front of him.

At 3:30 p.m., when the Confederates were in position to attack, they realized there was a strong Union force in their path. This altercation became significant because Sickles's III Corps was isolated from the rest of the army.

In moving Sickles had not only disobeyed Meade's orders but had left a sizeable gap in the Union line on Cemetery Ridge. When Meade realized what Sickles had done he was furious; however, before he could order the troops back to Cemetery Ridge, the Confederates attacked.

With this new alignment, the Confederates were forced to make readjustments in their own battle line, which created confusion on their behalf as well.

Much of the fighting around Devil's Den, Wheatfield and the Peach Orchard was chaotic for several reasons. 1) Difficult military maneuvers and skirmishes transpired over the same areas at different times during the day. 2) At least twenty brigades (both North and South) were fighting in this area from 4:00-7:30 p.m. 3) Other regiments within those brigades were constantly being shifted within the struggle to plug the holes.

(If the visitor has the time, park at Devil's Den and recreate the Confederate movement on Little Round Top by following the trail up through Big Round Top.)

Map 20

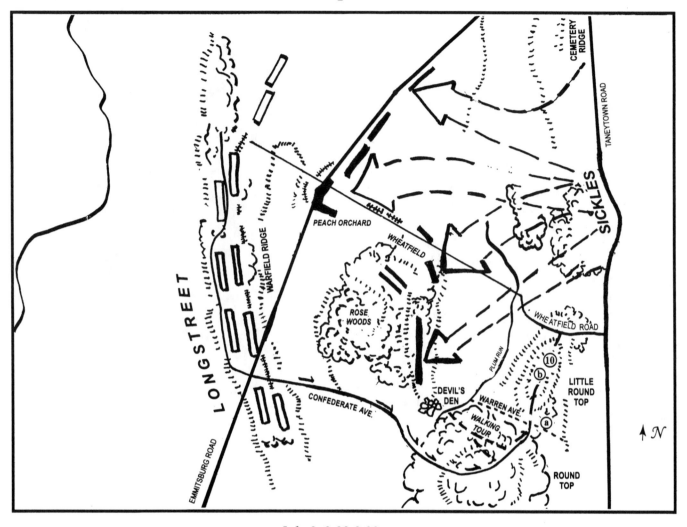

July 2, 2:00-3:00 p.m.
Major General Sickles redeploys his III Corps on the Emmitsburg road and
in the Peach Orchard/Devil's Den area.

THE STRUGGLE FOR LITTLE ROUND TOP AND DEVIL'S DEN

4:00-6:30 p.m.

The contest opened with Longstreet's cannon firing on the Peach Orchard/Devil's Den sector. For approximately half an hour the Union and Confederate artillery dueled.[50] To avoid the incoming shells, the Confederate infantry lay down in the woods. One Arkansas private's "nerves cracked under the strain. Each time a Federal shell roared past his head, he leapt to his feet, ran a few yards and fell face down in the scalding dust only to repeat the performance every few minutes."[51] The private was soon subdued by one of the officers of the regiment. An incoming round struck within the Arkansas regiment. It killed a captain, "hit the ground, ricocheted, severed the right arm of the Orderly Sergeant, tore off the Third Sergeant's head, mangled a corporal's leg and shrieked off through the trees."[52]

After the bombardment Major General John B. Hood's Confederate division launched their attack (see map 21).

Shortly after the assault began, Hood was wounded and taken to the rear. Later, due to this injury, he lost the use of his left arm.

Major General John B. Hood

Go to Stop 10a: Little Round Top, 20th Maine Monument, Sykes Avenue/Warren Avenue.

Map 21

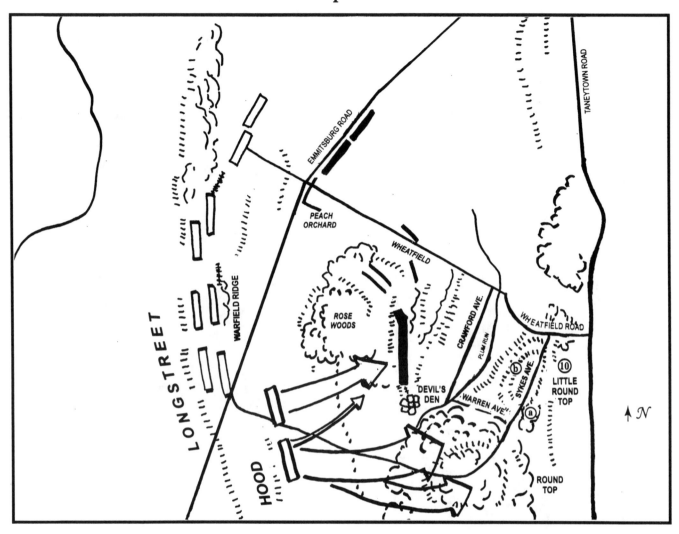

Hood's Division begins its assault on Devil's Den and Big Round Top.

Stop 10a: Little Round Top, 20th Maine Monument
(Gettysburg National Park Stop 8)

Approximately 4:45-6:30 P.M.

Confederate Commanders: vs. **Union Commander:**

Brigadier General Evander Law

Colonel Strong Vincent*
(1,300 men)

Brigadier General Jerome Bonaparte Robertson
(2,134 men)**

*Vincent was mortally wounded July 2nd on Little Round Top.
**This number is reached by adding two regiments from Law's brigade and three regiments from Robertson's brigade.

Colonel William Oates

Colonel Joshua Chamberlain

As the battle for Little Round Top continued, the contest in and around the Rose Woods, Wheatfield, Devil's Den and Peach Orchard was raging.

The 15th Alabama, approximately 499 men commanded by Colonel William Oates, was on the far right of the Confederate battle line. At the summit of Big Round Top he halted his troops in order to take a brief respite.

On the Union side, Colonel Strong Vincent's brigade was hurried into position to the southern end of Little Round Top. The far left of his line was commanded by Colonel Joshua Chamberlain and his 20th Maine regiment, approximately 360 men. One week before the battle of Gettysburg Chamberlain was given command of the regiment. As the combat began on Little Round Top, Vincent strongly advised him, "This is the left of the Union line. You understand. You are to hold this ground at all costs."[53]

With only a few minutes to prepare, the Maine men built a crude defensive position. The combination of the incline and numerous rocks made the position quite formidable (see map 22).

Suddenly, descending from Big Round Top, the 15th Alabama struck. Chamberlain saw that his left wing was being flanked. Therefore, while under fire, he maneuvered his left flank at right angles

Map 22

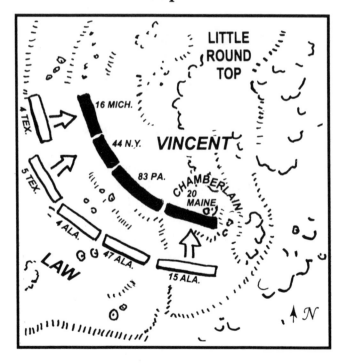

Little Round Top
(20th Maine Monument)
The Alabama troops attack.

with the original line (see map 23). As Chamberlain recalled:

> *the edge of conflict swayed to and fro, with wild whirlpools and eddies. At times I saw around me more of the enemy than of my own men; gaps opening, swallowing, closing again with sharp convulsive energy; squads of stalwart men who had cut their way through us...All around, [a] strange, mingled roar...*[54]

Again the Alabama troops charged up the hill. A Maine man reached out to grab the Confederate flag, only to be bayonetted through the head.[55] The noise of the battle was terrific. Orders from the officers could not be heard, but Rebel yells resounded all along the line. There were strange animal sounds and the grotesque sounds of skulls being struck by musket butts. The red-gray, smokey haze was blinding.[56] Four to five times the rugged Alabama troops rushed upon the 20th Maine. The number of dead and wounded rose with each new assault. Casualties covered the ground and blood stood in puddles among the rocks.[57] Nearly out of ammunition and determined not to give up his position, Chamberlain later wrote:

> *It was imperative to strike before we were struck by this overwhelming force in a hand-to-hand fight, which we could not probably have withstood or survived. At that crisis, I ordered the bayonet. The word was enough. It ran like fire along the line, from man to man, and rose into a shout...*[58]

Like a swinging gate, the left wing of the 20th Maine smashed into the exhausted Confederates. The rest of the regiment soon followed (see map 24). Even though Chamberlain was wounded (once in the right instep and bruised on his left thigh), he accompanied his men in the charge. One Alabama

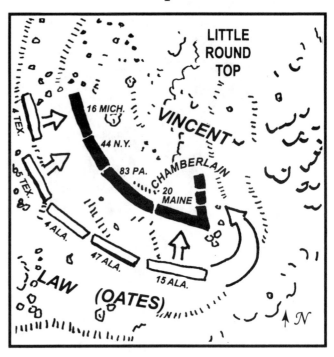

Map 23

Little Round Top
(20th Maine Monument)
Colonel Chamberlain positions his regiment at right angles to meet the Confederate assault.

officer discharged his revolver in Chamberlain's face; he missed and immediately handed Chamberlain his sword and surrendered. With great self-control, he accepted the officer's weapon.[59]

In and around this location Chamberlain counted 150 dead and wounded Confederates. The 20th Maine suffered 120 dead and wounded, 270 in this small area.

Go to Stop 10b: The Summit of Little Round Top, Sykes Avenue

Map 24

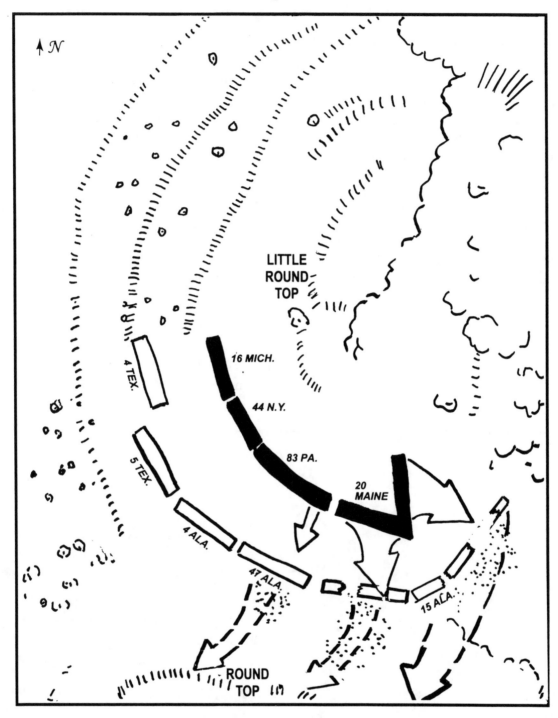

Little Round Top
(20th Maine Monument)
The 20th Maine, assisted by the 83rd Pa., fix bayonets and charge.
The Confederates retreat to the Devil's Den area.

Stop 10b: Little Round Top, 140th New York Monument.

While the fighting continued to seesaw near the 20th Maine, the right flank of Vincent's brigade was also being threatened. Two Texas regiments had been pressing the troops near the crest. Private John C. West, 4th Texas Regiment, was one of these Confederates assailing the western slope of Little Round Top. A bullet passed through his beard, struck a rock, then shattered and cut his lip; this was the only wound West received that day.[60]

The Union's right flank was on the verge of crumbling. Colonel Patrick H. O'Rorke's 140th New York rushed in as reinforcements (see map 25). Without halting at the summit, the 140th made their way down through the rocks. O'Rorke led the attack shouting, "Down this way, boys!...Here they are men, commence firing!"[61] A Confederate sighted O'Rorke and fired. The bullet passed through his neck killing him. Many New Yorkers, however, saw the man and fired upon him. After the battle someone counted seventeen holes in this individual.[62]

It was now around 6:30 p.m. On Little Round Top approximately 1,124 Confederate and Union soldiers were either killed or wounded.

The Union cannon on Little Round Top belonged to Lieutenant Charles E. Hazlett's battery. Pulling the cannon up the steep hill was difficult.

LITTLE ROUND TOP
The topographical significance of the hill.

From Little Round Top: The Wheatfield and Peach Orchard.

From Little Round Top overlooking the Union line:
In the upper right hand corner is Cemetery Hill and Cemetery Ridge.

From Little Round Top:
In the distance is Seminary Ridge and the field where the Confederates crossed during the final assault.

Yet, with determination and aid from some infantrymen, the artillerymen placed their cannon at the crest. The guns, however, could not be used effectively to the immediate front; yet, their presence boosted the morale of the troops fighting on Little Round Top.

During the struggle Hazlett rushed to his friend Brigadier General Stephen H. Weed, who had been wounded and lay dying. Hazlett bent over his comrade, and they spoke privately for a few minutes. Suddenly Hazlett, shot in the head, toppled over on the general. Weed later died at a field hospital.

Map 25

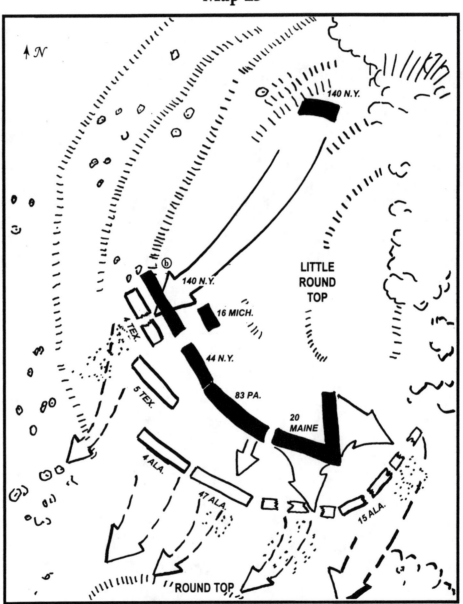

Little Round Top
(140th N.Y. Monument)
The 140th N.Y. charges from the north over the western slope of Little Round Top. Colonel O'Rorke is shot and killed where the 140th N.Y. Monument now stands.

Post-war photo:
Private John C. West

Colonel Patrick H. O'Rorke

Lieutenant Charles E. Hazlett

Brigadier General Stephen Weed

EXCURSION ON LITTLE ROUND TOP
THE PENNSYLVANIA RESERVES AS REINFORCEMENTS

July 2, sometime after 6:30 p.m.

Five Southern brigades finally drove the Union forces from the vicinity of Devil's Den, Rose Woods, Wheatfield and Peach Orchard. To check them, the Pennsylvania Reserves charged down into the Valley of Death and met the Confederates on the next ridge.

They were

fighting at their own homes, and in defense of all that was dear to them. They had also just been informed of the death of their...commander, Gen. Reynolds, and as they charged upon the enemy

the cry, "Revenge for Reynolds," rang out above the din . . .[63]

The Pennsylvania troops struck the line and a brief struggle ensued at the stone wall on the edge of Houck's Ridge. Exhausted from two hours of fighting and low on ammunition, the Confederates abandoned their assault on Little Round Top, and the Pennsylvania Reserves returned to the defenses around the hill.[64]

Along the length of the Valley of Death, approximately 840 Confederate and Union soldiers were killed or wounded (see map 26).

Go to Stop 11a: East-Devil's Den, Slaughter Pen Area, Crawford Avenue.

THE DEVIL'S DEN
Two views of east-Devil's Den

The name Devil's Den predated the Battle of Gettysburg. In fact, the actual name "Devil's Den" does not refer to the huge boulders in this area, but to a small cave/den which is within the larger rocks.

Map 26

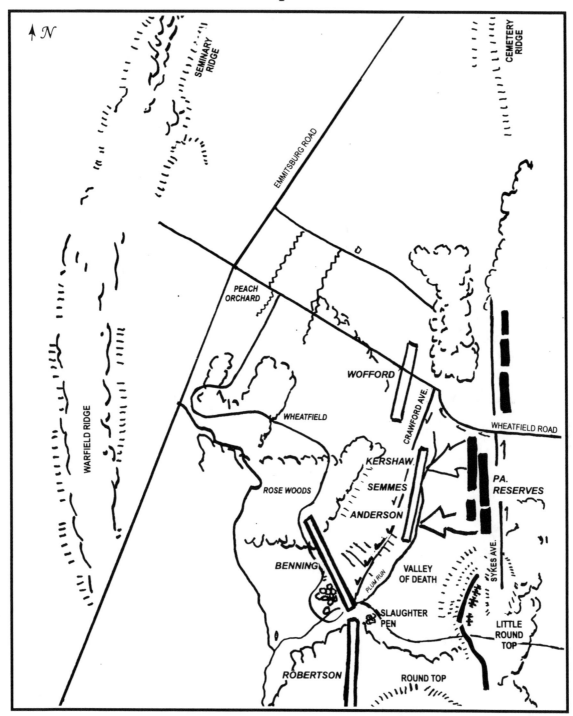

Little Round Top

The Pennsylvania Reserves charge across the "Valley of Death" and stop the Confederate advance. Approximately 840 soldiers are either killed or wounded in this valley.

Stop 11a: East-Devil's Den, Slaughter Pen Area.

THE BATTLE FOR THE EAST SIDE OF DEVIL'S DEN, SLAUGHTER PEN, AND PLUM RUN

July 2, First Stage: approximately 4:30-5:00 p.m.

Confederate Brigade Commanders: vs.   Union Brigade Commander

Brigadier General Evander Law

Brigadier General J. H. Hobart Ward
(2,188 men)

Brigadier General Jerome B. Robertson
(1,527 men)*

* This number is reached by adding two regiments from Law's brigade and two regiments from Robertson's brigade.

Colonel William F. Perry

Colonel Elijah Walker

Brigadier General Henry Benning
(1,420 men)

Just prior to the initial shots at Little Round Top, the 4th Maine, which was facing toward Big Round Top, was attacked by two Confederate regiments. Colonel W.F. Perry, commander of the 44th Alabama, described the scene.

As the line emerged from the woods into the open space...sheet of flame burst from the rocks less than a hundred yards away. A few scattering shots in the beginning gave warning in time for my men to fall flat, and thus largely to escape the effect of the main volley. They doubtless seemed to the enemy to be all dead; but the volume of the fire which they immediately returned proved that they were very much alive.[65]

The Maine men checked the first assault. At a range of about twenty paces, the Alabama troops stood up and returned fire. They exchanged fire for twenty-minutes, or more (see map 27).[66]

Map 27

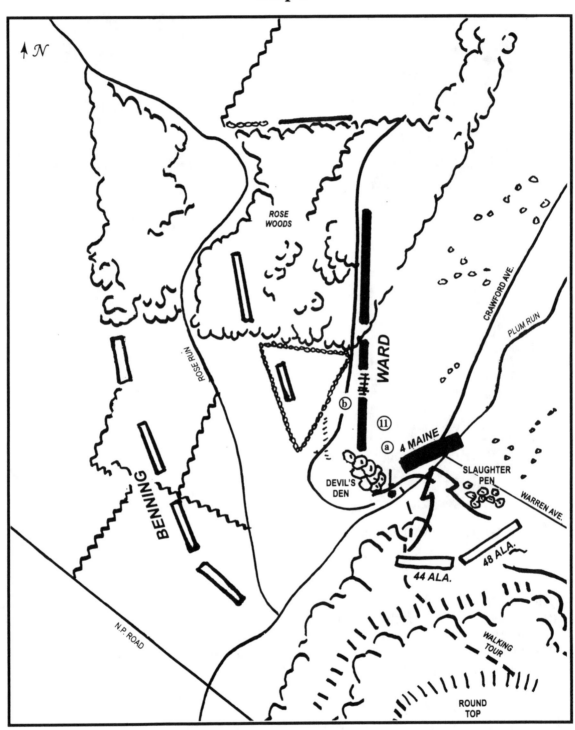

July 2 , 4:30-5:00 p.m.
East-Devil's Den

EAST-DEVIL'S DEN: SLAUGHTER PEN, PLUM RUN AREA

July 2, Second Stage: approximately 5:00-7:00 p.m.

Arriving on the scene, the brigade of Confederate Brigadier General Henry L. Benning joined in the attack at Devil's Den.

Overwhelmed, and seeing the Confederates closing in on the four cannon on top of Devil's Den, Colonel Elijah Walker of the 4th Maine ordered his regiment to fix bayonets and charge up Devil's Den. With their aid and that of the 124th New York, the Union guns were saved and the battle continued (see map 28).[67]

To replace the 4th Maine on the line, two other regiments (40th New York and 6th New Jersey) were rushed into the Slaughter Pen, Plum Run area. Here the battle lingered as the troops on top of Devil's Den defended the three cannon.[68]

In the Slaughter Pen area nearly 200 Alabama soldiers were either killed or wounded.

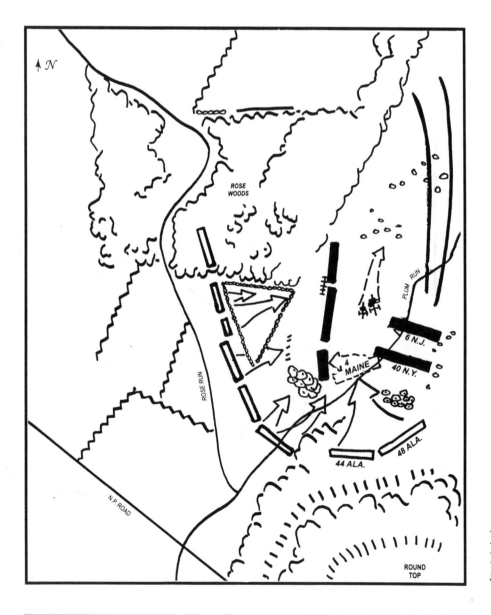

Go to Stop 11b:
West-Devil's Den,
4th New York Battery,
Sickles Avenue.

Map 28
East-Devil's Den,
5:00-5:30 p.m.

Stop 11b: West-Devil's Den, 4th New York Battery Monument.

WEST-SIDE DEVIL'S DEN, HOUCK'S RIDGE

First Stage: 4:30-5:00 p.m.

At the top of Devil's Den, facing southwest, there were initially four cannon assigned to Captain James E. Smith's 4th New York Independent Battery. To the right of the battery the 124th New York and three other regiments of Brigadier General J. H. Hobart Ward's brigade were deployed. Two cannon, however, were placed in the valley leaving four on top of Devil's Den (see map 29).

During the first attack the 1st Texas charged this area. Smith recalled the scene.

I never saw the men do better work; every shot told; the pieces were discharged as rapidly as they could be with regard to effectiveness, while the conduct of the men was superb; but when the enemy approached to within three hundred yards of our position the many obstacles in our front afforded him excellent protection for his sharpshooters, who soon had our guns under control.[69]

Held in check, the Texans and New Yorkers continued to exchange volleys. Seeing the cannon

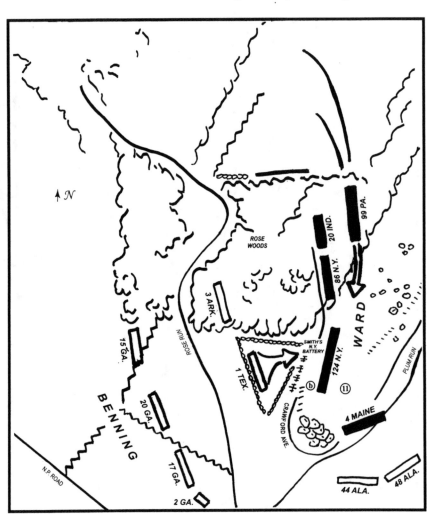

Map 29
West-Devil's Den,
4:00-5:00 p.m.

Captain James Smith

Colonel Augustus Van Horne Ellis

Major James Cromwell

Post-war photo as colonel:
Captain Charles Weygant in center

in danger of being captured, Colonel Augustus Van Horne Ellis, of the 124th New York (along with part of the 4th Maine), ordered his regiment to fix bayonets and charge. Mounted on his horse, the 124th's Major James Cromwell waved his sword over his head and shouted the charge. The New Yorkers rushed after their major and knocked the Texans back about 200 yards. Captain Charles Weygant, an officer of the 124th New York, described the assault.

Roaring cannon, crashing riflery, screeching shots, bursting shells, hissing bullets, cheers, shouts, shrieks and groans were the notes of the song of death which greeted the grim reaper, as with mighty sweeps he leveled down the richest field of scarlet human grain ever garnered on this continent.[70]

Yet, just as the New Yorkers pushed the Texans back, Benning's Georgia brigade arrived with reinforcements and smashed into the Union line.

WEST-SIDE DEVIL'S DEN, HOUCK'S RIDGE

Second Stage: approximately 5:00-5:30 p.m.

Benning's 1,420 soldiers counter-attacked, along with the remnants of the other Confederate regiments. Cromwell was shot through the heart and fell from his horse. Ellis shouted, "My God! My God, men! Your Major's down; save him! save him."[71] The 124th continued to battle the onrushing Confederates. Ellis rose in his stirrups and raised his sword; a bullet pierced his forehead, and he toppled to the ground. Overwhelmed and exhausted the 124th New York and the remnants of Ward's brigade slowly retreated.

The 124th initially had 238 men. Captain Weygant could only locate 100 of the New Yorkers; 85 had either been killed or wounded. The rest were missing. Ward's brigade had taken into battle 2,188 troops. The entire brigade suffered 758 casualties (see map 30).

The 1st Texas and 20th Georgia were given credit for capturing three Union cannon. The fourth one had been taken away during the first stage, shortly after the Confederates attacked. However, the 20th Georgia lost their colonel during the melée. While leading his regiment, Colonel John A. Jones had half his head torn away by a shell fragment.[72] Out of 350 men engaged, the 20th Georgia lost approximately 121 killed and wounded. The 1st Texas began with 426; they ended with 333.

Go to Stop 12: The Wheatfield, Sickles Avenue.

Map 30

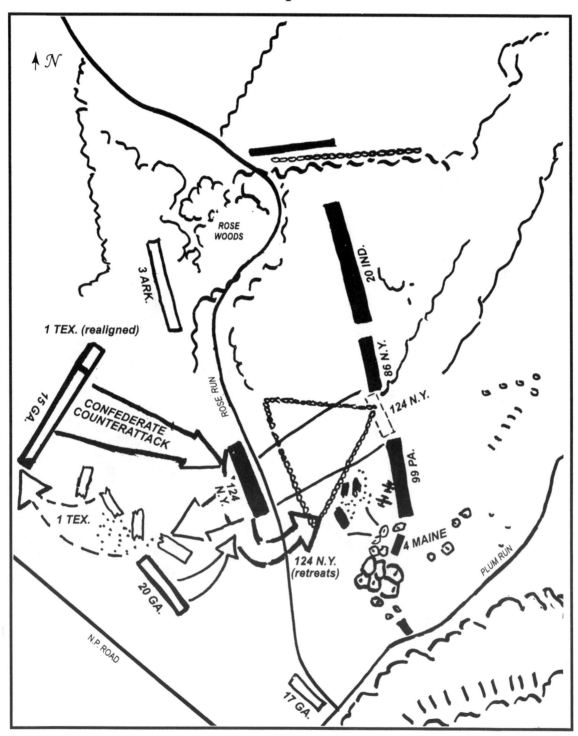

West-Devil's Den,
5:00-5:30 p.m.

Stop 12: Wheatfield
(Gettysburg National Park Stop 9)

*WHEATFIELD

July 2, First Stage 5:00-5:30 p.m.

Confederate Brigade Commander: vs.   **Union Brigade Commander:**

**Brigadier General George T. Anderson
(1,874 men)**

**Colonel P. Regis de Trobriand
(1,708 men)****

*The Wheatfield and the woods surrounding it were described as the "whirlpool." At least eleven Confederate and Union brigades fought in this area from 5:00-7:00. After the first stage time became approximate. Therefore, excluding the first stage, the estimated time is not given.

**The number of men that Colonel de Trobriand had directly under his command was 1,387; however, two Union regiments (8th New Jersey and 115th Pennsylvania) were sent to reinforce de Trobriand's position. Shortly after the first attack these two regiments were forced to retreat—to avoid being flanked by the Confederates.[73]

As Benning's brigade began its assault on Devil's Den, Brigadier General George T. Anderson's Confederate brigade launched its first attack near the Wheatfield. Hiding behind trees, rocks and fences Colonel P. Regis de Trobriand's troops met them (see map 31). De Trobriand later recalled the initial contest.

It was a hard fight. The Confederates appeared to have the devil in them...On the other side, my men did not flinch...when their assailants descended into the ravine and crossed the creek they were received, at a distance of twenty yards, with a deadly volley, every shot of which was effective. The assault broken, those who were on the opposite slope began a rapid fire at a range still very short. On both sides, each one aimed at his man, and, notwithstanding every protection from the ground, men fell dead and wounded with frightful rapidity.[74]

Due to their natural defensive position and the tenacity of the Union troops, the Confederates were unable to dislodge them. Consequently, Anderson withdrew his men in order to rest, regroup and await reinforcements.

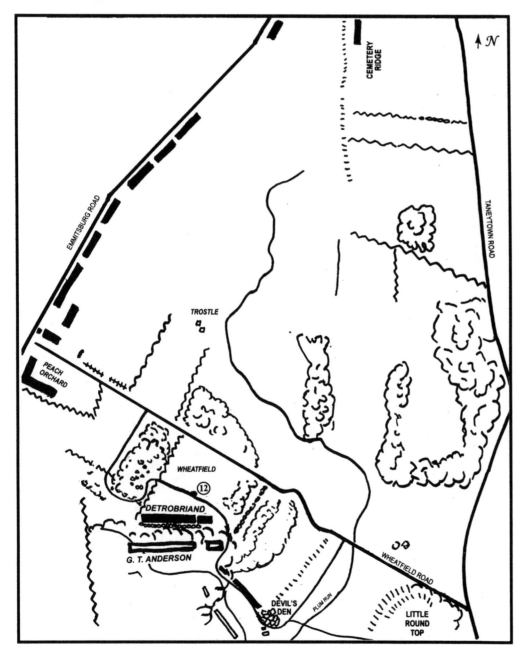

Map 31
Wheatfield
First stage
5:00-5:30 p.m.

WHEATFIELD

Second Stage

Confederate Brigade Commanders: vs.   **Union Brigade Commanders:**

Brigadier General George T. Anderson
(2,779 men)*

Colonel P. Regis de Trobriand
(1,387 men)**

Brigadier General Joseph B. Kershaw
(1,262 men)***

Colonel William S. Tilton
(655 men)

Colonel Jacob B. Sweizer
(1,010 men)

*Part of the 1st Texas and 3rd Arkansas joined General Anderson's brigade after assaulting Devil's Den. However, after the first stages, all the brigades' numbers became approximate. During the lull, Anderson was hit by a bullet in the thigh and was carried to the rear. He survived his wound.

**In the first stage several of Colonel de Trobriand's regiments were repositioned to Devil's Den in order to aid General Ward's brigade. Consequently, the number of men in de Trobriand's sector was much less, approximately 718 men.

***Only three South Carolina regiments attacked at the Wheatfield during this time, the 15th, 7th and 3rd.

By the time the second stage commenced, two more Union brigades had been placed in the area of the Wheatfield.

Having sent for reinforcements, Anderson's Georgia brigade, along with Brigadier General Joseph B. Kershaw's South Carolina brigade, attacked. Three South Carolina regiments (the 15th, 7th, and 3rd) fought Colonel William S. Tilton's brigade. The three remaining South Carolina regiments attacked near the Peach Orchard area. (This will be discussed at Stop 13.)

Colonel de Trobriand and Colonel Tilton's brigades caught the brunt of the renewed assault. Tilton's right flank was exposed and outflanked by the South Carolinians. Consequently his brigade withdrew. That retreat compelled Colonel Jacob Sweitzer to remove his Union brigade from the Wheatfield, while de Trobriand's regiments continued to defend their ground. Without the support of the other two brigades, however, his men (the 17th Maine, 5th Michigan and 110th Pennsylvania) were forced to flee through the Wheatfield (see map 32).

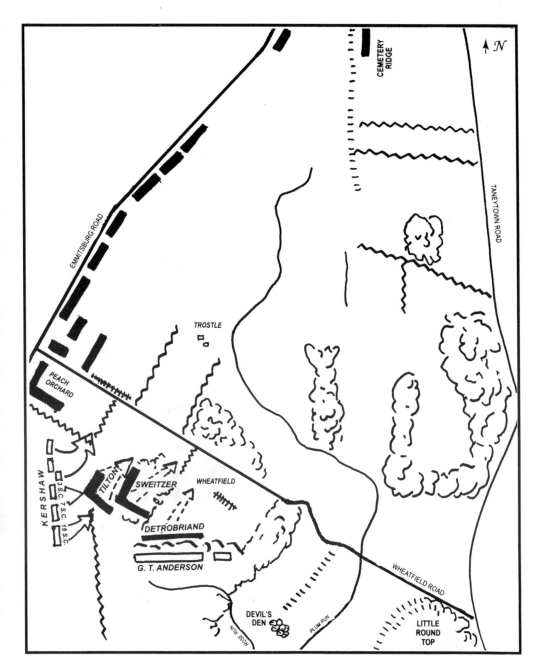

Map 32
Wheatfield
Second Stage
Tilton's brigade
flanked; the Union
brigades retreat.

WHEATFIELD

Third Stage

Confederate Brigade Commanders: vs.   **Union Brigade Commanders:**

Brigadier General George T. Anderson
(2,779 men)

*Colonel Edward E. Cross
(853 men)

Brigadier General Joseph B. Kershaw
(1,262 men)

Colonel Patrick Kelly
(532, known as The "Irish Brigade")

**Brigadier General Samuel K. Zook
(975 men)

*Upon entering the area of the Wheatfield, Colonel Edward Cross was shot in the abdomen by a Confederate sniper. He was carried to a field hospital where he died. His dying words were, "I did hope I should see peace restored to our distressed country. I think the boys will miss me. Say goodbye to all."[75]

**While positioning his brigade, Brigadier General Samuel Zook was also shot in the abdomen. He fell from his horse and was taken to the rear. He died the next day, Friday, July 3.[76]

After the Confederates drove the three brigades out of the Wheatfield sector, three more Union brigades were rushed into the area, with a fourth waiting in reserve (see map 33).

The three fresh Union brigades struck the two Confederate brigades and there was a short, furious struggle. Colonel Patrick Kelly's Irish Brigade, and Brigadier General Samuel Zook's brigade, engaged the South Carolinian troops. Major St. Clair A. Mulholland (of the 116th Pennsylvania, one of the regiments in the Irish Brigade) recalled the initial fight in the Wheatfield.

. . . [A]lthough the ground was covered with huge boulders, interspersed with forest trees, hilly and rough, the alignment was well preserved and, as it neared the crest, met the enemy and received a volley. But the shots were too high and did but little damage and the men rushed on. Soon the lines were but a few feet apart, and the men returned the fire with deadly effect. Captain Nowlen drew his revolver and opened fire; nearly all the other officers followed his example. Little Jeff Carl killed a man within six feet of his bayonet. That hero, Sergeant Francis Malin, was conspicuous by his dash and bravery, as his tall form towered above all around him — a noble soul. He soon fell dead with a bullet through his brain.[77]

In charging, the Irish Brigade ran straight into the South Carolinians. The firing stopped. Officers and men on both sides looked at each other; the Confederates still held their rifles. Finally, Mulholland yelled, "Confederate troops lay down your arms and go to the rear!" Many South Carolinians were captured.[78] The rest of Kershaw's brigade fell back to regroup and await reinforcements.

Before the Confederates launched another offensive, Major Mulholland reflected on the aftermath of the short melée. He described it at a later date.

When the regiment charged and gained the ground on which the enemy stood, it was found covered with their dead, nearly every one of them being hit in the head or upper part of the body. Behind one large rock five men lay dead in a heap...One of them, in his dying agony, had torn his blouse and shirt open, exposing his breast and showing a great hole from which his heart's blood was flowing.

Major St. Clair A. Mulholland

Captain Garrett Nowlen

...in the immediate front one could see the enemy massed and preparing for another attack. The dead of the One Hundred and Tenth Pennsylvania Volunteers lay directly in front, on the ground which that command had vacated but a half hour before, and one young boy lay outstretched on a large rock with his musket still grasped in his hand, his pale, calm face upturned to the sunny sky, the warm blood flowing from a hole in his forehead and running in a red stream over the gray stone.[79]

For fifteen or twenty minutes the two lines rested and waited. Then the Confederates, with the aid of reinforcements, struck the Wheatfield once again.

Map 33

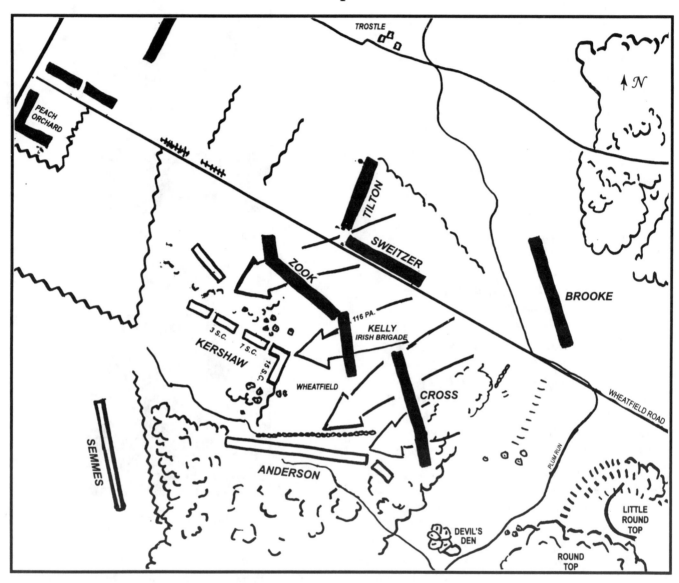

Wheatfield
Third Stage
Zook, Kelly and Cross attack across the Wheatfield.

WHEATFIELD

Fourth Stage

Confederate Brigade Commanders: vs.   Union Brigade Commanders:
       (7,694 men)   (2,358 men)

Brigadier
General
George T.
Anderson
(2,779 men)

Colonel
John R.
Brooke
(851 men)

*Brigadier
General
Paul J.
Semmes
(1,334 men)

Brigadier
General
Joseph B.
Kershaw
**(2,183 men)

Colonel
Patrick
Kelly
(532 men)

Brigadier
General
William T.
Wofford
(1,398 men)

Brigadier
General
Samuel
Zook
(975 men)

*Brigadier General Paul Semmes was wounded in the thigh. He later died from this injury.
**Kershaw's entire brigade now turned toward the Wheatfield.

As the Confederates renewed their attack, Colonel John R. Brooke's brigade relieved Cross's brigade which had been acting as the reserve. The 27th Connecticut commanded by Lieutenant Colonel Henry C. Merwin (a regiment in Brooke's brigade), unleashed a deadly fire upon the Confederates when they were within twenty-five yards of them. However, their commander, shot in the chest, pitched headlong into the dust. As he went down, Merwin cried out, "my poor regiment is suffering fearfully".[80] The 27th Connecticut sustained heavy losses. Out of 75 men engaged, 38 were lost.

Brooke's brigade maintained the line for a short time. Yet, caught in a deadly cross-fire, they were forced to back slowly out of the Wheatfield.

While Brooke's brigade contended with the Confederates at the southern section of the Wheatfield, the Irish Brigade and Zook's brigade were struck by the South Carolinians, one Georgia regiment and Brigadier General William T. Wofford's fresh detachment.

Overwhelmed, fatigued, and out of ammunition, the two Union brigades retreated. However, the killing in the Wheatfield continued in one final stage (see map 34).

**Lieutenant Colonel
Henry C. Merwin**

Map 34

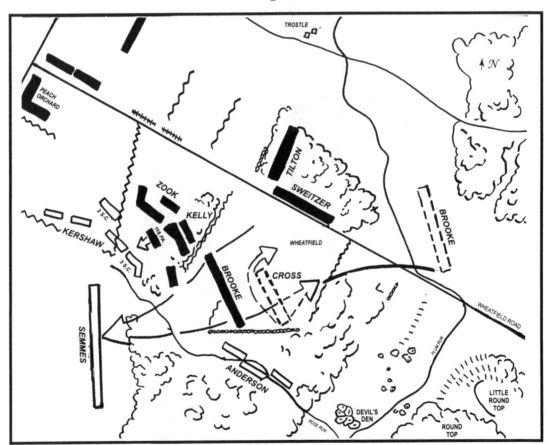

Wheatfield
Fourth Stage
Brooke relieves Colonel Cross's brigade.

WHEATFIELD

Fifth Stage

Confederate Brigade Commanders: vs.   Union Brigade Commander:

Brigadier
General
George T.
Anderson
(2,779 men)

Colonel
Jacob B.
Sweitzer
(1,010 men)

Brigadier
General
Paul
Semmes
(1,334 men)

Colonel
Harrison
Jeffords

Brigadier
General
Joseph B.
Kershaw
(2,183 men)

Lieutenant
Michael
Vreeland

Brigadier
General
William T.
Wofford
(1,398 men)

Nearly 7,694 Confederates were approaching the Wheatfield. During the fifth stage of fighting, the Union troops were outnumbered by approximately 6:1. That occurred primarily because Sweitzer was mistakenly under the impression that his brigade was acting as reinforcements and not as a replacement brigade. He noted Union troops retreating, but he continued to deploy in the Wheatfield and the surrounding hills. Brigadier General James Barnes, Sweitzer's commanding general, saw the situation and sent a message to Sweitzer to abandon the Wheatfield. The message was never received (see map 35).[81]

The Union troops soon realized that they were being fired upon from three sides. Colonel Harrison Jeffords, commander of the 4th Michigan, saw their national flag lying in the middle of the Wheatfield. Colonel Jeffords, his brother, and Lieutenant Michael Vreeland ran to recover it. At the same moment several Confederates rushed for the flag. A vicious melée ensued. One Confederate grabbed the flag; Jeffords' brother struck him in the neck with his sword. The brother then took a minié ball in the chest, but Major Jarius Hall killed the man who shot him. Vreeland was shot in the chest and right arm, and another Confederate struck him in the head with his clubbed musket.

The national flag was retrieved, and his brother and Vreeland survived their wounds. However, Colonel Jeffords was mortally wounded. One account stated he was bayonetted in the chest. It was recorded that Jeffords cried, "Mother, mother, mother!" and then died.[82]

Severely outnumbered, the Union troops withdrew from the Wheatfield. The Confederates finally succeeded in capturing this ground. The price was high on both sides. Among the Confederate and Union soldiers there were approximately 4,000 casualties in the Wheatfield and the surrounding woods. The 4th Michigan lost 165 men out of 342. The Irish Brigade took 532 men into battle; 198 were either killed, wounded or missing. Out of 1,262 South Carolinians, in the three regiments, 303 were either killed or wounded.

In the meantime, in the Peach Orchard, the Union troops could hear the initial assaults in the Wheatfield. When the second stage of the Wheatfield began the first stage of the Peach Orchard commenced.

Go to Stop 13: Peach Orchard, Wheatfield Road.

Map 35
Wheatfield
Fifth Stage
Sweitzer's brigade isolated
in the Wheatfield.

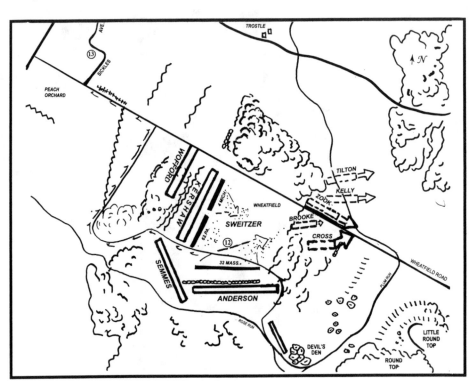

Stop 13: Peach Orchard, Wheatfield Road/Sickles Ave.
(Gettysburg National Park Stop 10)

PEACH ORCHARD

July 2, First Stage: approximately 5:30-6:00 p.m.

Confederate Commander: vs.   **Union Commander:**

Brigadier General Joseph B. Kershaw
*(971 men)

Brigadier General Charles K. Graham
(1,516 men)

Turning north, three South Carolina regiments charged the twenty-four Union cannon which were facing south parallel to the Wheatfield road. One of these Union batteries (six cannon in each battery) was Battery B, 1st New Jersey Artillery, commanded by Captain A. Judson Clark. The New Jersey men fired shell and canister into the onrushing Confederates (see map 36).

Having only canister left, Sergeant William Clairville directed Sergeant Ellis Timm to fire into the Confederates. Michael Hanifen, acting as the number five man of Battery B, later recalled the pandemonium.

...the colors fell, making a beautiful gap in their line, which was closed up and on they came. Capt. Clark passed from gun to gun, animating and

---

*Recall, three South Carolina regiments were fighting in the Wheatfield. The 2nd and 3rd Battalions and the 8th South Carolina troops attacked near the Peach Orchard.

Map 36

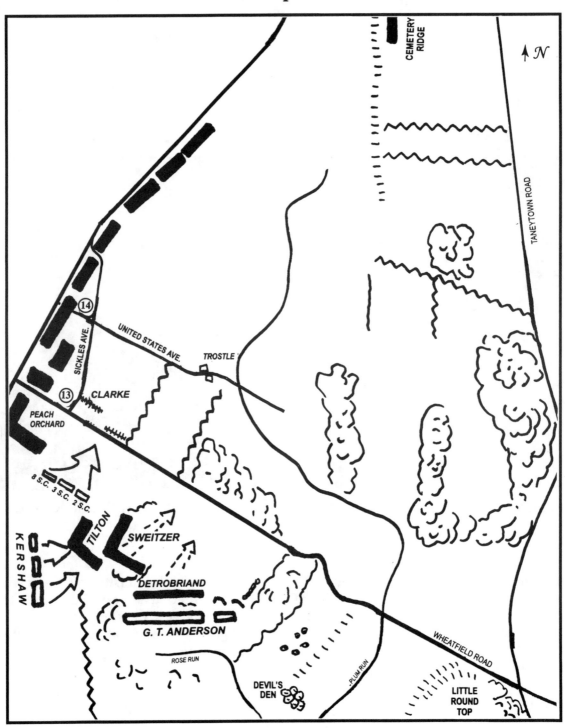

Peach Orchard
First Stage
5:30-6:00 p.m.
Three South Carolina regiments attack the Union cannon near the Peach Orchard.

encouraging the men, as cool and calm as if it was a battery drill...I handed the next two canisters to Elias Campbell, each containing 76 balls, he said, "This is the stuff to feed them; 'tis good for them; feed it to their bellies, Timm; mow them down, Timm." And Timm aimed to hit them in the middle of their anatomy, and they fell like grass before a mower's scythe.[83]

The initial attack was broken, and the South Carolina troops took cover behind a slight incline near the Wheatfield. There they regrouped and waited for reinforcements.

BATTERY B
1ST NEW JERSEY ARTILLERY

Captain A. Judson Clark

Sergeant Ellis Timm

Sergeant William Clairville

Michael Hanifen

PEACH ORCHARD

Second Stage: approximately 6:00 p.m.

Confederate Brigade Commanders: vs.   **Union Brigade Commander:**

*Brigadier General William Barksdale
(1,620 men)

**Brigadier General Charles K. Graham
(1,516 men)

Brigadier General Joseph B. Kershaw
(971 men)

Brigadier General William T. Wofford
(1,398 men)

*Later in the fight Brigadier General William Barksdale was mortally wounded in the chest.

**During the struggle, Brigadier General Charles K. Graham was wounded and taken prisoner.

Prior to the third and fourth stage at the Wheatfield, the second stage at the Peach Orchard occurred.

The South Carolinians' respite was brief. On their left flank Brigadier General William Barksdale's Mississippi brigade smashed into the Peach Orchard. Captain Theodore Malloy of the 8th South Carolina remembered the charge (see map 37).

The order was given. We began the fatal charge, and soon had driven the enemy from their guns in the orchard, when a command was given to 'move to the right,' which fatal order was obeyed under a terrible fire, thus leaving the 'Peach Orchard' partly uncovered. The enemy soon rallied to their guns and turned them on the flank of our brigade. Amid a storm of shot and shell from flank and front our gallant old brigade pushed towards the Round Top, driving all before them, till night put an end to the awful slaughter.[84]

Out of 215 men, the 8th South Carolina lost 100, nearly half.

Meanwhile, at the Peach Orchard, Graham's small brigade attempted to check the Mississippians. The 2nd New Hampshire was one of the Union regiments deployed in the Peach Orchard. They poured a brisk fire into the Confederates, but this had little effect. The Confederate advance continued blazing away at the soldiers.

Lieutenant Edmund Dascomb of the 2nd New Hampshire was shot dead. Captain Joseph A. Hubbard was hit in the forehead and wandered aimlessly into the Confederate lines living for more than two hours. The 2nd New Hampshire had taken 354 men into battle and suffered 193 casualties.[85]

Overwhelmed, the Union troops were forced to relinquish the Peach Orchard. Barksdale then turned his Mississippi brigade north, and Wofford continued on toward the Wheatfield.

Casualties around the Peach Orchard numbered at least ,958 Union and Confederate soldiers killed or wounded.

Captain Theodore Malloy   **Lieutenant Edmund Dascomb**   **Captain Joseph A. Hubbard**

VIGNETTE ON HENRY WENTZ AND HIS FAMILY

John and Mary Wentz lived in a small house near the Peach Orchard (see map 37). As one account stated, in 1852, their son, Henry Wentz, moved South. At the outbreak of the Civil War, Henry joined the Southern army. During the battle of Gettysburg Henry served as an artillerist in a unit deployed near his ancestral home.

Mrs. Wentz and Susan, her daughter, left the house during the battle; John stayed to protect the property from looters. After the battle, on July 3, Henry Wentz carefully made his way back to his family home. There, he found his father asleep in the basement. Before he left he wrote a note. "Goodbye, father; God bless you, Henry."[86]

Go to Stop 14:
Intersection of Sickles
Avenue and United
States Avenue

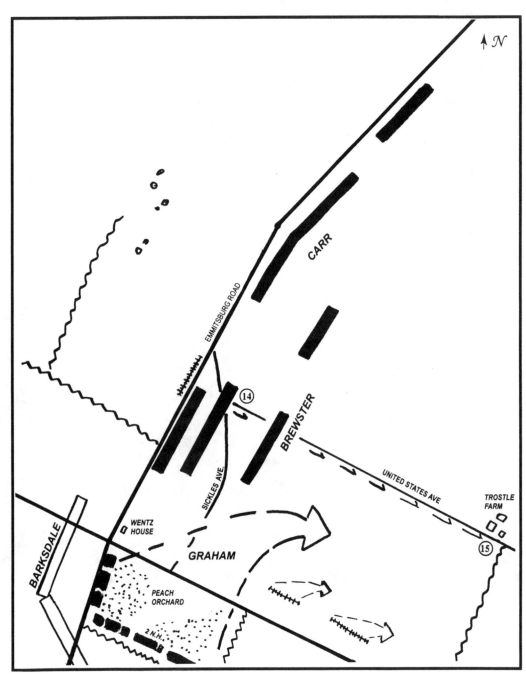

Map 37
Peach Orchard
Second Stage
6:00

Stop 14: Intersection of Sickles Avenue and United States Avenue

THE STRUGGLE ON EMMITSBURG ROAD

Confederate Brigade Commanders: vs.   Union Brigade Commanders:

Brigadier General William Barksdale
(1,837 men)

Colonel William Brewster
(1,620 men)

Brigadier General Cadmus M. Wilcox
(1,726 men)

Brigadier General Joseph B. Carr
(1,800 men)

Colonel David Lang
(742 men)

Turning north, the Mississippians struck the left flank of the Union line on the Emmitsburg Road. At the same time two additional brigades attacked from the west. One regiment which met the Mississippians was the 11th New Jersey, commanded by Colonel Robert McAllister. While rallying his men, the colonel was hit by a bullet in the left thigh. Major Philip Kearney, next in command, was then shot in the knee. (McAllister survived his wound; however, Major Kearney died on August 9, 1863.) In just a few minutes the 11th New Jersey suffered the fall of five commanders, either killed or wounded. To encourage the New Jersey troops, Corporal Thomas Johnson and the color guard were ordered to carry the colors (flags) twenty paces in front of the regiment.

The 11th New Jersey held its line for a short while, but, like the other Union regiments, it could not check the onrushing Confederates. Slowly it retreated to Cemetery Ridge (see map 38).

The 11th New Jersey lost 141 killed and wounded, and 12 missing, 153 out of 275 engaged.[87] Along the Emmitsburg road, approximately 3,722 Confederate and Union troops were either killed or wounded.[88]

Colonel Robert McAllister

Major Philp Kearney

Go to Stop 15: Trostle Farm, on United States Avenue.

Map 38

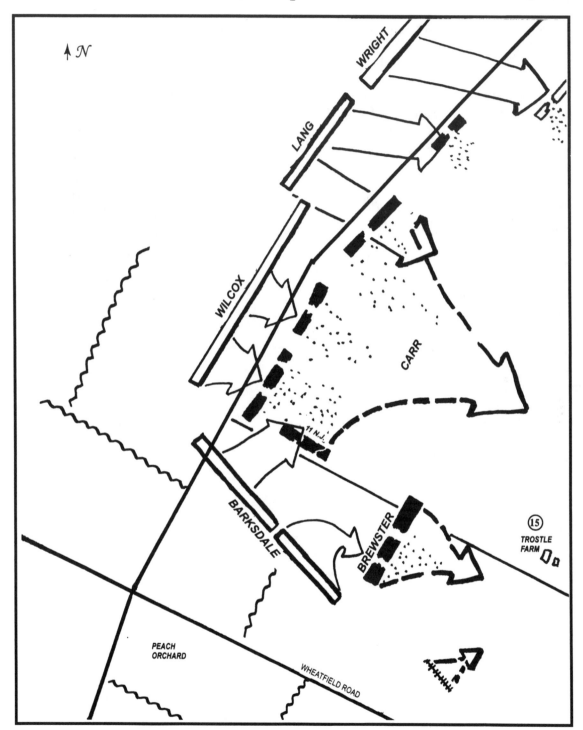

Confederates clear the Peach Orchard — Emmitsburg Road area.

Stop 15: Trostle Farm

To protect the Union retreat, Captain John Bigelow of the 9th Massachusetts Battery was ordered to place his six cannon around the Trostle farm (see map 39). When the Mississippians were within fifty yards of the cannon the artillerymen fired canister into their midst. Several times they were repelled, but they pressed on and outflanked the cannon. Bigelow recalled the scene.

> *I then saw the Confederates swarming in on our right flank, some standing on the limber chests and firing at the gunners, who were still serving their pieces; the horses were all down; overhead the air was alive with missiles from batteries, which the enemy had now placed on the Emmetsburg [sic] Road...I then gave orders for the small remnant...to fall back.*[89]

The Confederates shot the horses so that the Union cannon could not be pulled back to the rear. Consequently, four cannon were captured by the Mississippi brigade.

The 9th Massachusetts Battery suffered 26 killed and wounded out of 104 engaged. Forty-five horses were killed around the Trostle barn and house.

Captain John Bigelow

Go to Stop 16: Father Corby's Statue, on Hancock Avenue before the Pennsylvania Monument.

Map 39

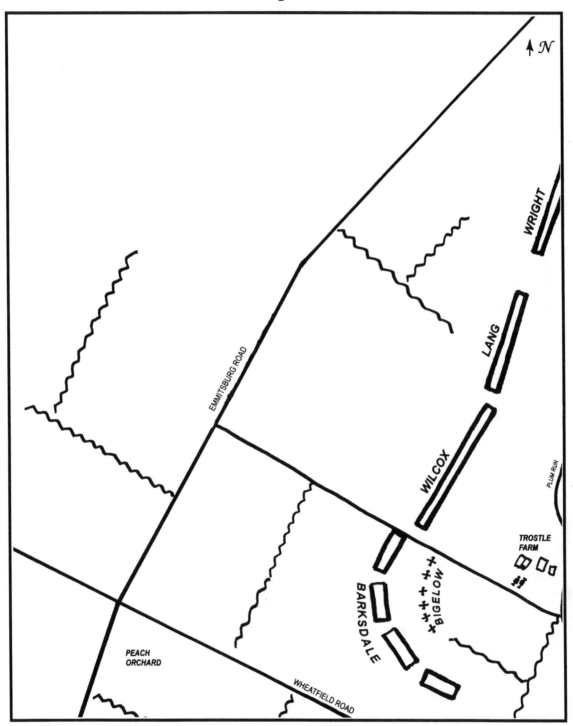

Trostle Farm
Bigelow's 9th Massachusetts Battery delays Barksdale's brigade.

TROSTLE FARM

Captain John Biglow's 9th Massachusetts battery rushes into action near the Trostle farm.

With most of the horses shot down the 9th Massachusetts battery is only able to take two cannon off the field.

Stop 16: Father William Corby's Statue

VIGNETTE PERTAINING TO THE IRISH BRIGADE,
(PRIOR TO THE BATTLE IN THE WHEATFIELD)

Before the Irish Brigade was sent into the Wheatfield to help check the Confederates, Father Corby pronounced absolution. He said,

Dominus noster Jesus Christus vos absolvat, et ego, auctoritate ipsius, vos absolvo ab omni vinculo, excommunicationis interdicti, in quantum possum et vos indigetis deinde ego absolvo vos, a pecatis vestris, in nomini Patris, et Filii, et Spiritus Sancti. Amen.[90]

Translation: May the Lord Jesus Christ absolve you, and I in his name absolve you from all your chains, with the exception of ex-communication. And by how much I am able I absolve you from your sins and mistakes, in the name of the Father, Son, and Holy Spirit, Amen.

Father Corby

Go to Stop 17: 1st Minnesota/Pennsylvania Monuments, Hancock Avenue.

Stop 17: 1st Minnesota/Pennsylvania Monuments
(Gettysburg National Park Stop 12)

OPPOSING COMMANDERS AT THE CENTER

Third Confederate Corps Commander: vs.   **Union II Corps Commander:**

Lieutenant General Ambrose P. Hill

Major General Winfield Hancock

Brigadier General Cadmus Wilcox
(1,700 men)

Colonel William Colvill, Jr.
(269 men)

Brigadier General Ambrose Wright

Colonel Paul J. Revere

After the four Confederate brigades pushed aside the Union troops along the Emmitsburg road, the defeated units fell back to Cemetery Ridge. The Confederates now moved toward the breach which had been left in the Union line by Sickles' III Corps (see map 40). Major General Winfield Hancock, commander of the II Corps, realized the urgency of stopping them. He ordered three New York regiments to attack Barksdale's Mississippi brigade. Suffering from heavy casualties, low on ammunition, and fatigued, the Mississippians retreated back to Seminary Ridge.

Hancock then went in search of infantry to check Brigadier General Cadmus Wilcox's Alabama brigade of approximately 1,700 men.[91] He located the 1st Minnesota, only 262 men, and shouted to their colo-

Map 40

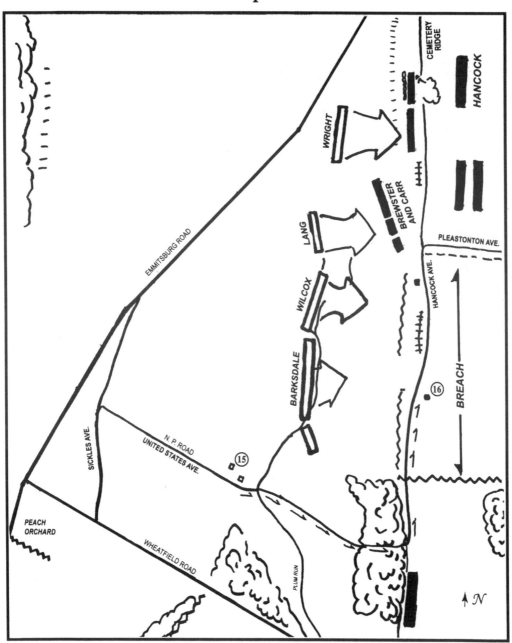

The Confederates breach the Union line.

nel, William Colvill, Jr., "Advance Colonel, and take those colors."[92] The ridge had to be held at all costs, even if it meant the sacrifice of the regiment to gain the time needed for reinforcements to arrive. The 1st Minnesota advanced until they neared the ravine (see map 41). Suddenly, "Charge!" rang out along the line, and, with a rush, they ran headlong into the Alabama brigade.

Bullets whistled past the Union troops; shells screeched overhead; canister fell all about them. Comrade after comrade dropped from their ranks. No one had time for a second look at the fallen; they had no time to weep.[93] Colonel Colvill fell, shot in the foot. The Confederates engulfed the 1st Minnesota and sent a deadly enfilading fire into their ranks, but the Union artillery poured shot and shell into the Alabama brigade. Even without the aid of the Union reinforcements, the Alabama brigade was checked and fell back to Seminary Ridge.

The price was high for the 1st Minnesota. Out of 262 soldiers, 215 lay among the dead and wounded. On July 3, 24 of the remaining 47 were either killed or wounded.[94] Of their 1,700 men, the Alabama brigade lost 577 killed or wounded.[95]

Brigadier General Ambrose Wright's Georgia brigade breached the wall toward the copse of trees on Cemetery Ridge. (see map 41). But Union reinforcements poured into this area and forced them back to Seminary Ridge.

Aiding in Wright's repulse was the 20th Massachusetts commanded by Colonel Paul J. Revere, grandson of the Revolutionary War hero. It was during this struggle that shell fragments struck the colonel in the chest, mortally wounding him in his lungs. He died on July 5th.

By sunset the fighting on the Union left had subsided. Yet, on their right, the battle had only begun on Culp's Hill and east Cemetery Hill.

* * * *

Those visitors who would like a complete narration of the battle should continue to Culp's Hill and east Cemetery Hill (Stops 18-21). This part of the tour will take approximately twenty-five to thirty minutes.

Alternatively the visitor may continue to Cemetery Ridge, Stop 22, the intersection of Hancock Avenue and Pleasonton Avenue.

Those who must forgo this part of the tour should be aware that the fighting on Culp's Hill was significant. If the right flank of the Union Army had been taken the Confederates might have been able to defeat the Army of the Potomac at Gettysburg and possibly change the outcome of the war. Eleven hours of fighting took place upon this hill from July 2 to July 3.

Go to Stop 18: Spangler's Spring, Slocum Avenue

Map 41

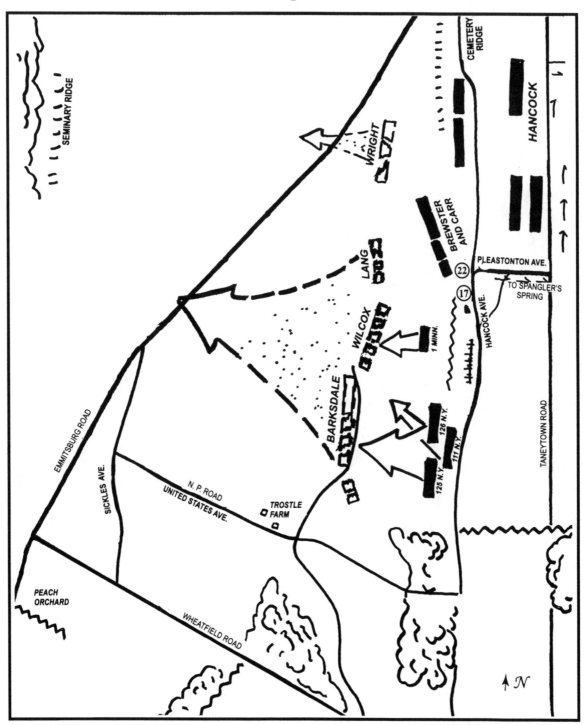

Three New York regiments and the 1st Minnesota help repulse the Confederate attack on Cemetery Ridge. Wright's and Lang's brigades are thrown back as well.

Stop 18: Spangler's Spring, Excursion.
(Gettysburg National Park Stop 13)

MURDER IN THE MEADOW

THE 2ND MASSACHUSETTS AND 27TH INDIANA ATTACK ACROSS THE MEADOW

Friday July 3, Around 7:00 a.m.

Colonel Silas Colgrove   **Lieutenant Colonel Charles Mudge**

Before the visitor proceeds to Culp's Hill and continues with the battle on the night of July 2, it is necessary to discuss the engagement in this area.

★ ★ ★ ★

About 7:00 a.m., the Union troops, deployed in the woods southwest of the meadow, attacked the Confederate trenches at the base of Culp's Hill (see map 42).

When Colonel Silas Colgrove, of the 27th Indiana, heard the order to charge across the meadow he anxiously pulled at his nose and stated to himself, "It cannot be done, it cannot be done." Lieu-

Map 42

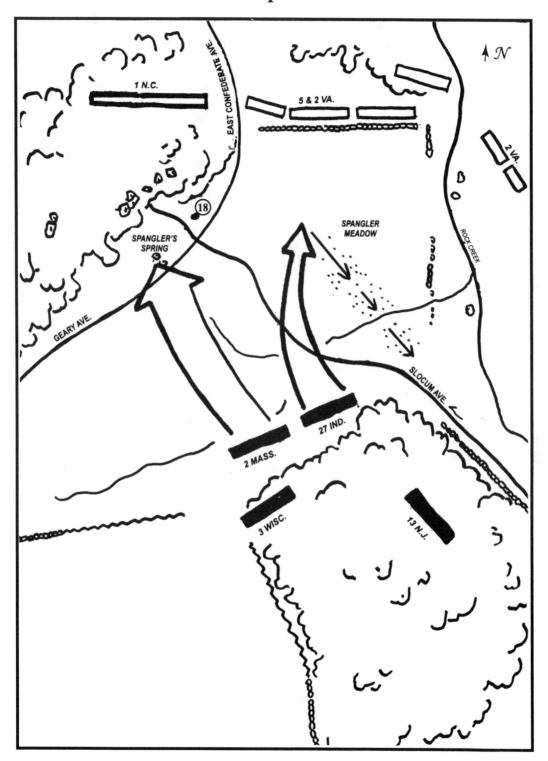

Spangler's Spring
2nd Massachusetts and 27th Indiana charge across Spangler's Meadow.
Nearly 200 soldiers fell in this attack.

tenant Colonel Charles Mudge, of the 2nd Massachusetts, also doubted the wisdom of the directive and declared, "It is murder, but it is the order." Then he said, "Up, men, over the works; Forward, Double-quick!"[96]

From the 1st North Carolina post the 2nd Massachusetts was on the right and the 27th Indiana was deployed on the left. The two regiments began crossing the meadow and advanced toward the Confederates (see map 42). When they were approximately half-way into the meadow, the Confederates let lose a well-aimed, well-timed volley and briefly broke up the lines. Corporal E. R. Brown, of the 27th Indiana, later recalled the event.

The air was alive with singing, hissing and zipping bullets.... The line also continued to advance, though not rapidly. Men stepped to the front as they loaded, then halted to take aim and fire.[97]

The 27th, caught in a deadly cross-fire, turned back to their original position; however, the 2nd Massachusetts was able to reach the Confederate breastworks. Nevertheless, when the Indiana troops fled the field, the 2nd Massachusetts was hit by the devastating cross-fire, and they too retreated.

The order for this charge had been a blunder in generalship and had achieved no strategic goal.[98]

Corporal E. R. Brown

The 27th lost 112 killed or wounded. The 2nd Massachusetts suffered 130 killed or wounded, and 242 Union lay upon the meadow bed, including Lieutenant Colonel Mudge who was shot in the throat and fell in the middle of the field.

VIGNETTE CONCERNING WESLEY CULP, MEMBER OF THE 2ND VIRGINIA THE "STONEWALL" BRIGADE

Culp was a common name in and around Gettysburg in the 1800's. Wesley Culp was born in York Springs, Pennsylvania, and like Henry Wentz, Wesley moved south prior to the war. At the outbreak of the Civil War, he also joined the Confederate Army. He returned to Gettysburg as a member of the famed "Stonewall Brigade," and on July 2nd he visited his sisters, who still lived in the town. On July 3, the 2nd Virginia helped repulse the attack made by the 27th Indiana and 2nd Massachusetts. The only man of the 2nd Virginia killed in action on that day was Wesley Culp, who died at the age of twenty-four near his cousin's farm.

Private Wesley Culp

Go to Stop 19: East-Culp's Hill; 137th New York Monument, Slocum Avenue, across from Brigadier General John W. Geary's statue, Geary's Avenue.

Stop 19: Culp's Hill, 137th New York Monument, Slocum Avenue/Geary Avenue

THE CONFEDERATE ASSAULT ON THE NORTHEAST PORTION OF CULP'S HILL

First Stage: July 2, 7:30-9:00 p.m.

Confederate Commanders: vs.   **Union Commander:**

*Brigadier General Francis R. Nicholls
(1,100 men)

Brigadier General George S. Greene
(1,350 men)**

Brigadier General John Jones
(1,600 men)

Brigadier General George Steuart
(1,700 men)

*Colonel Jesse M. Williams, however, led the Louisiana brigade during the battle because Nicholls had lost a foot at Chancellorsville.
**General Greene also received about 755 Union troops from other units and was holding them in reserve. In this sector, 4,400 Confederates engaged 2,105 Union soldiers.

The visitor should be aware that the numerous Union monuments lining Culp's Hill indicate the Union battle line on the evening of July 3. To follow the two opposing lines during the actual fight refer to the maps.

* * * *

The reason for the Union disadvantage on Culp's Hill was that, during the day, two Union brigades, which had been to the right of Brigadier General George S. Greene's brigade, had reinforced the line on Cemetery Ridge. Consequently, Greene guarded the Union's right flank with only 1,350 men and 755 in reserve. His brigade faced southeast and was stretched in a single line.

During the day the out-numbered troops worked quickly to build entrenchments and log breastworks. In addition, the numerous rocks, broken slopes, trees, and cliffs as steep as fifteen to twenty feet, acted as natural barriers. The combination made the Confederate attack more difficult.

Deployed on the far Union right was the 137th New York regiment, 423 men commanded by Colonel David Ireland, who were ordered to occupy the vacant trenches.

Assaulting the 137th New York was Brigadier General George Steuart's brigade numbering nearly 1,700 (see map 43). Since the attack began at a late hour, darkness and smoke soon enveloped Culp's Hill.

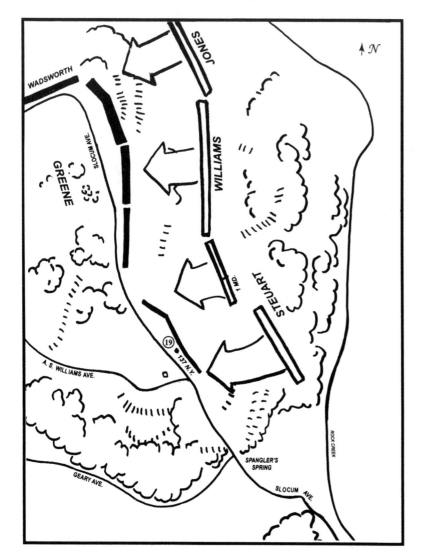

Map 43
Culp's Hill
July 2, 7:00 p.m.

One of the Confederates fighting in this area was Major W. W. Goldsborough of the 1st Maryland Battalion. He recalled that because of the poor visibility that night, they could not identify the breastworks and received a murderous volley from the Union position.[99] The main Confederate advance stalled; however, their left flank overpowered the 137th New York. To meet this threat Ireland placed his right flank at 90°. Sorely outnumbered, the New Yorkers reformed their battle line. To reinforce his right flank General Greene deployed his reserves. With their aid, the troops checked the Confederates in this area (see map 44). After four separate assaults on Culp's Hill, the intense fighting was over— around 9:30 p.m.[100] However, later in the evening, Captain Joseph H. Gregg, of the 137th New York, led a small skirmish against the Confederate position. While encouraging his men, Gregg fell mortally wounded.

Captain Joseph Gregg

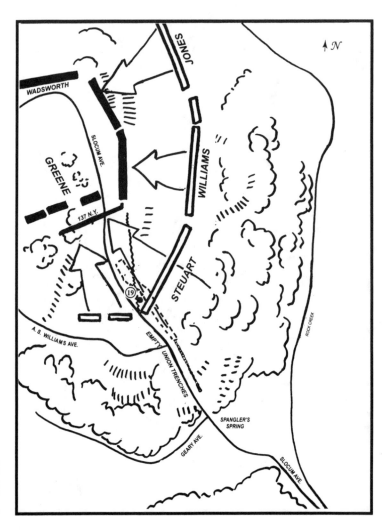

Map 44
Culp's Hill
July 2, 7:30-8:30 p.m.

By forcing the 137th New York right flank to turn, the Marylanders were able to capture the emptied Union trenches; the Confederates were then behind the Union lines. Hindered by darkness and needing reinforcements, the Confederate commanders decided to wait until daylight to capitalize on their success. By morning it was too late.

Sometime after 10:00 p.m., the Union brigades arrived back on Culp's Hill having helped to push back Wilcox, Lang, Barkskdale and Wright. They found their trenches occupied by Confederates. Unknowingly, several units marched right up to the breastworks. They were immediately met with a volley of musketry. For two more hours, scattered shots were heard throughout Culp's Hill. By midnight, both sides, exhausted and low on ammunition, settled down for the night (see map 45).

* * * *

While on Culp's Hill we will also discuss the battle on July 3, 4:30-11:00 a.m.

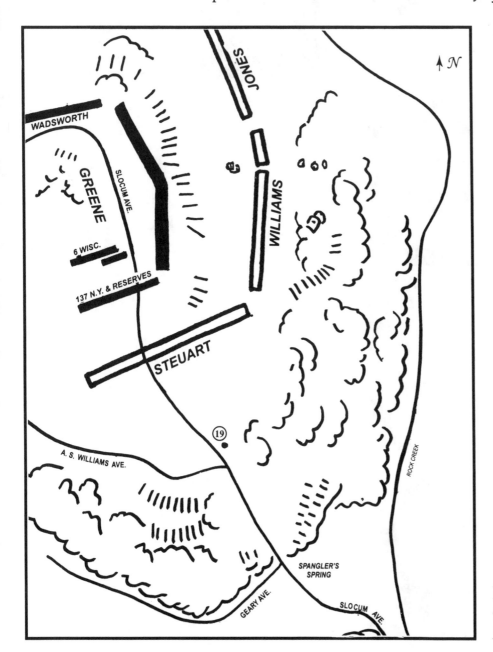

Map 45
Culp's Hill
July 2, 9:30 p.m.

EAST-CULP'S HILL

Second Stage: Friday, July 3, 4:30-11:00 a.m.

Confederate Commanders: vs.   **Union Commanders:**

Brigadier General
Francis R. Nicholls
(1,100 men)

Brigadier General
George S. Greene
(1,350 + 755
reinforcements)

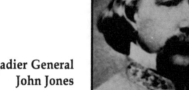

Brigadier General
John Jones
(1,600 men)

Colonel
Edward O'Neal
(992 men)

Brigadier General
Junius Daniel
(1,394 men)

Confederate Commanders: vs. **Union Commanders:**

Brigadier General
George Steuart
(1,700 men)

Brigadier General
Thomas Kane
(700 men)
(Pictured here in
Colonel's Uniform)

Colonel Charles Candy
(1,798 men)

Colonel
Archibald McDougall
1,835 men)

Brigadier General
Henry Lockwood
1,818 men)

Overall, approximately 6,800 Confederates were assaulting 8,300 Union troops.

Around 4:30 a.m. on Friday morning, Union cannon commenced firing on the entrenched Confederates. They suffered heavy losses during this bombardment but maintained their post. Many of the Confederate regiments were low on ammunition and resorted to searching the dead and wounded for their cartridge boxes.

At 5:00 a.m. the Confederate infantrymen opened fire on the Union line. The firing continued for two hours when the 27th Indiana and 2nd Massachusetts attacked across Spangler's meadow. Then, at approximately the same time, Brigadier General Henry Lockwood ordered the 1st Maryland, "Potomac Home Brigade," to charge the Confederate left flank near Spangler's Spring. The Marylanders pushed the Confederate skirmishers back but could not break their left flank. In just thirty minutes the Maryland regiment lost approximately 100 men, out of 674 (see map 46).[101] In this area Union and Confederate Marylanders fought one another.

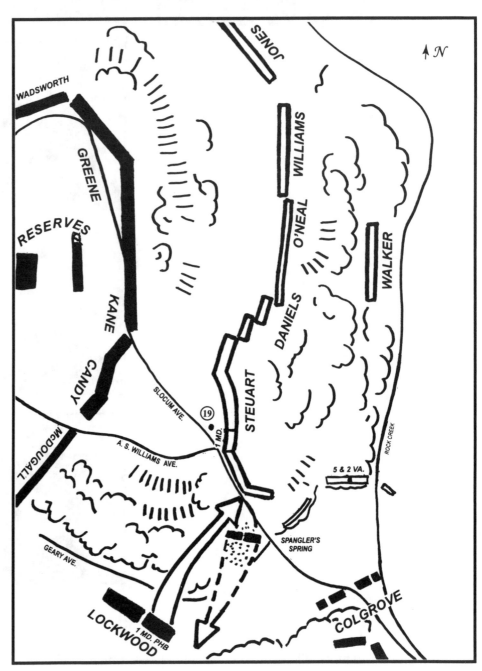

Map 46
Culp's Hill
July 3, 7:00 a.m.

Firing continued from both sides lined on Culp's Hill. As the battle raged, fresh Union troops arrived and joined in the fight.

In a deadlock, the ranking Confederate commander, Major General Edward Johnson, ordered Steuart to take the initiative and clear the woods of Union troops (see map 47). Steuart complied, yelling, "Attention! Forward, double-quick! March!" Goldsborough, of the Confederate 1st Maryland Battalion, remembered the doomed charge.

...[T]he little battalion of Marylanders, now reduced to about three hundred men...kept on, closing up its ranks as great gaps were torn through them by the merciless fire of the enemy in front and flank, and many of the brave fellows never stopped until they had passed through the

General Edward Johnson

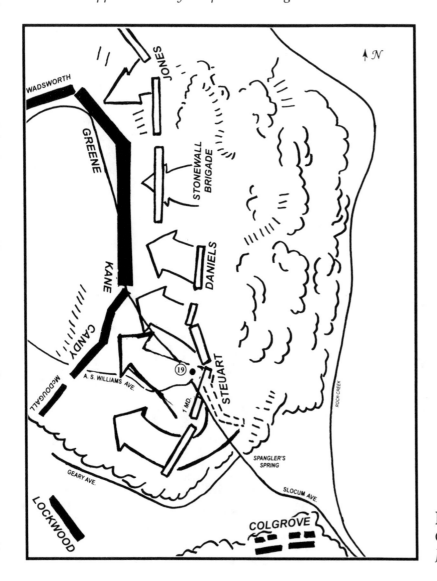

Map 47
Culp's Hill
July 3, 10:30-11:00 a.m.

enemy's first line or had fallen dead or wounded as they reached it.

But flesh and blood could not withstand that circle of fire, and the survivors fell back to the line of log breastworks...

General Steuart was heartbroken at the disaster, and wringing his hands, great tears stealing down his bronzed and weather-beaten cheeks, he was heard repeatedly to exclaim: "My poor boys! My poor boys!"[102]

Goldsborough was hit by a bullet in the chest. He survived his wound. Captain William H. Murray, who led the small battalion, was killed at the base of the Union entrenchments. One severely wounded Confederate Marylander raised himself to a sitting position and loaded his gun. The Union troops prepared to fire, but before they had the opportunity, the soldier placed his rifle near his head and with his ramrod pulled the trigger.[103]

Having fought eleven hours, exhausted both physically and emotionally, and out of ammunition, the Confederates fell back down the hill. A new battle line was established on the east side of Rock Creek. At the cost of heavy casualties, the Confederates failed to turn the right flank of the Union Army (see map 48).

Captain William H. Murray

The two days of fighting in this area cost the Union 1,085 men killed or wounded; the Confederates lost 1,609 for a total of 2,694 casualties.[104]

The forest on Culp's Hill was literally cut to pieces. In some trees up to 200 musket balls were found imbedded in their trunks. For nearly a half a century the forest on Culp's Hill stood desolate.[105]

CULP'S HILL

"The Meadow, near Spangler's Spring, from the Union position.
Looking toward Rock Creek."

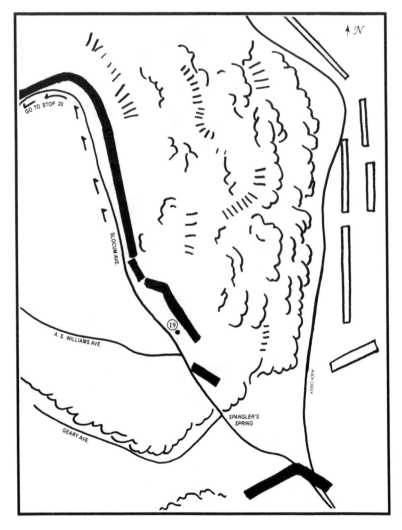

*Go to Stop 20: East-Cemetery Hill on
Baltimore Pike, near the Cemetery Gate.*

Map 48
Culp's Hill
July 3, 11:00 a.m.-evening

Stop 20: East-Cemetery Hill, near the Cemetery Gate.
(Gettysburg National Park Stop 14)

THE BATTLE FOR EAST-CEMETERY HILL

July 2, 8:00-10:00 p.m.

Confederate Commanders: **vs.**   **Union Commanders:**

Brigadier General Harry Hays
(1, 295 men)

Colonel Andrew Harris
(559 men)

Colonel Isaac Avery
(1,244 men)

Colonel Leopold Von Gilsa
(650 men)

While their comrades assailed Culp's Hill, Brigadier General Harry Hays and Colonel Isaac Avery deployed their Louisiana and North Carolina soldiers behind the slope in front of Cemetery Hill (see map 49). Awaiting them were two Union brigades which had suffered heavy casualties on the first day of fighting.

Rising up, the Louisiana "Tigers" and North Carolina "Tarheels" rushed across the field. Twenty-four Union cannon on Cemetery Hill and on Stevens' knoll to the south, spewed forth canister and shrapnel at a distance of only 700 yards (see map 49). Union infantry also poured volleys of musketry into the onrushing Confederates.

Colonel Avery was shot in the neck and fell from his horse. Before he died he wrote on a piece of scrap paper: "Tell my father I fell with my face to the enemy."[106]

Reaching the stone wall in front of Cemetery Hill, the Confederates used clubbed muskets and

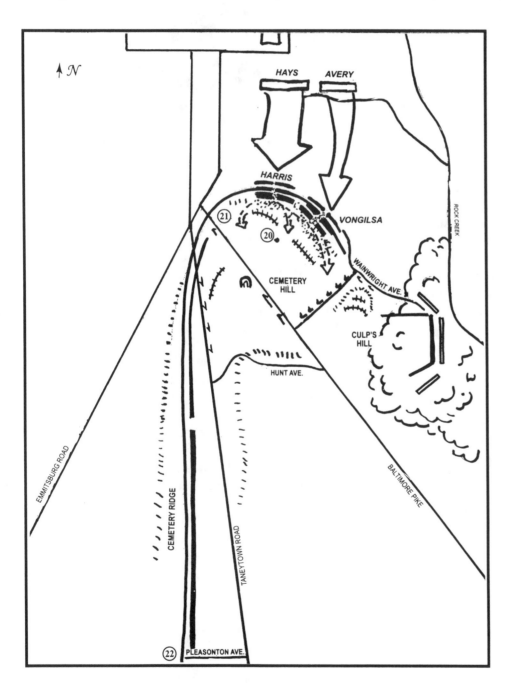

Map 49
East-Cemetery Hill
July 2, 8:00 p.m.

Colonel Harry Gilmor

Captain R. Bruce Ricketts

bayonets to breach the first Union line; the two infantry lines soon crumbled. The Louisiana troops rushed through the gap and approached the cannon on top of the hill. The artillerymen, however, put up a terrific struggle. One Confederate who participated in this confrontation was Colonel Harry Gilmor. He later recalled the horrible melée.

> *While advancing on the main line of works, I saw one of our color-bearers jump on a gun and display his flag. He was instantly killed. But the flag was seized by an Irishman, who, with a wild shout, sprang upon the gun, [but] he too was shot down. Then a little bit of a fellow, a captain, seized the staff and mounted the same gun; but...a ball broke [his] arm which held [the flag]...His third cheer was just heard, when he tottered and fell, pierced through the lungs.*[107]

One of the Union batteries being assailed by the Louisiana troops was the 1st Pennsylvania Light Artillery commanded by Captain R. Bruce Ricketts. He recalled that his men fought with handspikes, rammers, stones and pistols.[108]

To plug the gap, fresh Union reinforcements were rushed into this sector. Fighting now in the darkness, about two-hundred Confederates neared the Cemetery gate. The Union reinforcements came within twenty feet of them and fired a devastating volley. The Confederates staggered but fired back. For a short time the two sides engaged in hand-to-hand combat. Exhausted, bruised, and lacking reinforcements the Confederates were beaten back to their original position (see map 50).

The fighting on east Cemetery Hill was over around 10:00 p.m. on Thursday, July 2.[109] The killed and wounded in this area numbered about 625 Confederate and Union soldiers.

Map 50

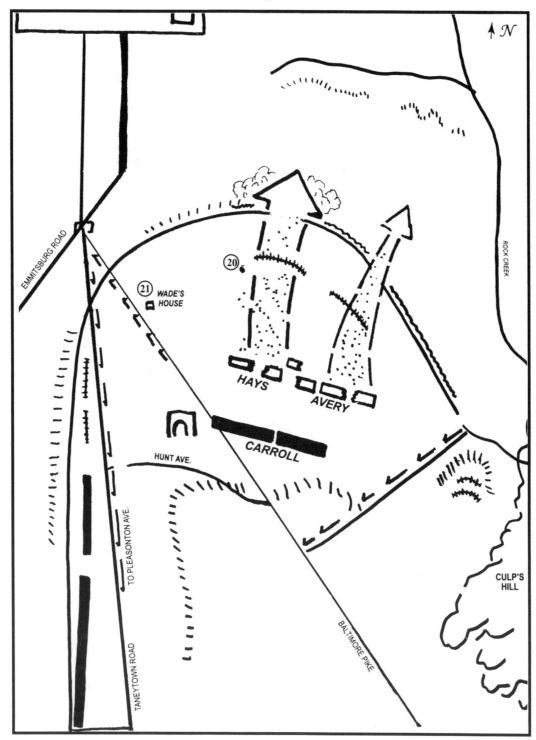

East-Cemetery Hill
July 2, 10:00 p.m.
Colonel S. S. Carroll's Union brigade drives the Confederates from the hill.

SUMMARY OF THURSDAY, JULY 2ND

Union Major General George Meade directed a defensive position along Cemetery Ridge, Cemetery Hill and Culp's Hill. General Lee planned to hit the Union line simultaneously on both flanks and in the center. After a hard day's fighting the Confederates occupied the Peach Orchard/Devil's Den area, but failed to take Little Round Top, Culp's Hill or east-Cemetery Hill, essentially the high ground commanding the area.

Military Analysis: Lee, after laying out the general plan, left the specific details of the action to his three corps commanders who did not discuss the timing of the attacks. Consequently, they struck the Union line at separate, uncoordinated intervals. The Union army, therefore, was able to transfer troops to the crisis areas and thwart the attacks.

Readdressing the analogy of the two fighters, the Confederate army was punching at the Union army. And, although the Union army fell to the mat, it was able to recover. The Confederates were never able to throw a full-force punch all along the Union line. In addition, the Union troops fought from a better vantage point and with a numerical advantage.

An estimate of casualties for the entire day (3:30 p.m.-12:00 a.m.) is 15,186 Americans either killed or wounded in nine-and-a-half hours of fighting (7,877 Union and 7,309 Confederates).

Go to Stop 21: Jennie Wade's house on the Baltimore Pike.

Stop 21: Jennie Wade's story.

"Jennie" Wade was a 20 year-old resident of Gettysburg. Her sister, who lived on Baltimore Street near Cemetery Hill, had recently had a baby. On the morning of July 3rd, Jennie was baking bread for the family when a stray bullet pierced through two pine doors and struck her in the back. She was killed instantly. Mary Virginia Wade was the only civilian killed during the three day battle.

Jennie Wade

Go to Stop 22: The Intersection of Pleasonton Avenue and Hancock Avenue.

| Stop 22: Intersection of Pleasonton Avenue and |
| Hancock Avenue, Cemetery Ridge |

THE FINAL ASSAULT

Friday, July 3

THE ARMY OF NORTHERN VIRGINIA:

Lee's initial strategy for July 3 was fairly simple. At dawn his troops on Culp's Hill would resume their attack. Simultaneously, their main force would strike Cemetery Hill and Cemetery Ridge—near the copse of trees. Meanwhile, Major General Stuart's cavalry, having arrived late at Gettysburg Thursday afternoon, would ride around the Union army and strike at its rear (see map 51).

THE ARMY OF THE POTOMAC:

Meade met with his subordinate generals Thursday night and decided to maintain the defensive position and await a Confederate assault. The Union line was shaped like a fishhook. Culp's Hill was the barb, Cemetery Hill the hook, and Cemetery Ridge the shank. Little Round Top/Big Round Top were an extension of the shank. During the morning of July 3, Meade and Hancock, in charge of the Union line on Cemetery Ridge, discussed the probability of an attack on his position.[110]

FRIDAY MORNING

After the Union force preempted the attack, the Confederates resumed their assault on Culp's Hill. After five hours of hard fighting, the struggle for Culp's Hill ended with the Union right flank still secure.

Due to poor communications and inadequate generalship, the other Confederate troops did not simultaneously attack the Union center. Yet Lee was determined to make his main assault there. In order to weaken the line, Lee ordered a massive cannonade to precede the infantry assault.

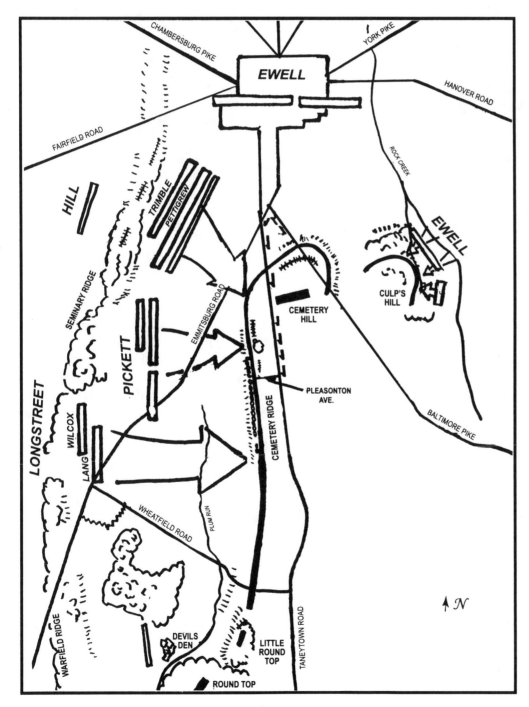

Map 51
Cemetery Ridge
July 3
Lee hoped to make a
three-pronged attack,
the main thrust coming
at the center
of the Union line.

THE ARTILLERY DUEL

July 3, 1:00-3:00 p.m.

Confederate Artillery Commander: **vs.**   **Union Artillery Commander:**

Colonel E. P. Alexander

Brigadier General Henry Hunt

Around 1:00 p.m., one hundred and forty-two cannon opened fire on the Union troops. In the northern section of the Confederate line ten cannon concentrated their fire on the twenty-nine cannon deployed on Cemetery Hill. In the center, one hundred and three cannon opposed thirty-one Union guns. Near the Peach Orchard twenty-eight cannon dueled with forty-three Union cannon which were stationed from Little Round Top to the intersection of Hancock and Pleasanton Avenues. The Union Artillery reserve was positioned near Taneytown Road and was ready to replace damaged cannon along the line (see map 52).[111]

The Confederate barrage was designed to demoralize the infantry on Cemetery Ridge and destroy the cannon. After disrupting the Union line, the Confederates planned for their infantry to break through the Union center, to be followed closely by reinforcements to smash the entire line.

The Union goal was less intricate: destroy the Confederate guns and create havoc.

After the cannonade began, the entire valley filled with smoke, making visibility poor. Consequently, both sides overshot their targets. One Union officer speculated that nine-tenths of the Confederate shells fell behind the infantry lines on Cemetery Ridge.[112] It was actually safer for the men on the ridge than for the troops stationed behind the lines near Taneytown road. To protect themselves, they lay behind the stone wall. Most of the projectiles passed harmlessly overhead; however, at times they exploded among the men. The 111th New York, deployed near Bryan's farm, received an incoming shell which exploded in their midst killing seven.[113]

Nearly 5,000 Union troops were crowded in this area. They were hot in their wool uniforms and had little water or food. A few troops started toward the rear but were subdued by a lieutenant who drew his sword and ordered them to return to their posts.[114]

Map 52

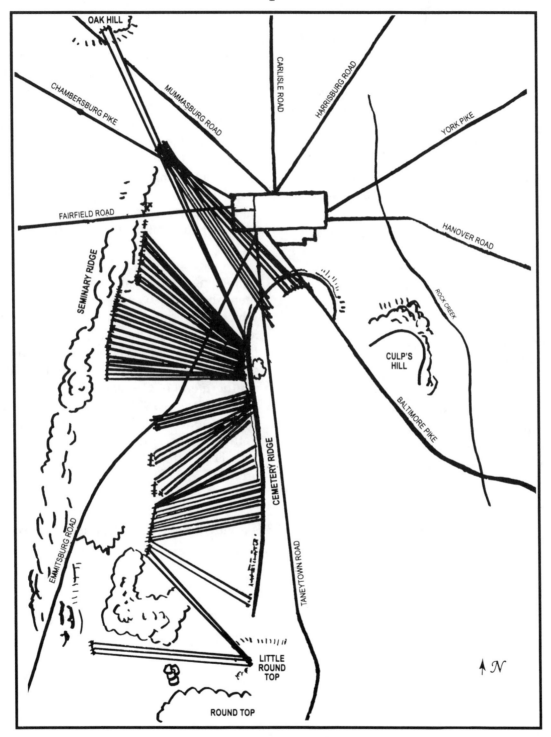

Cemetery Ridge
The cannonade,
1:00-3:00 p.m.

On Seminary Ridge the situation was reversed. Since the Union artillerymen were unintentionally firing over the Confederate cannon, the troops deployed behind Seminary Ridge suffered severe casualties. Sergeant-Major David E. Johnston, 7th Virginia, recalled the scene:

> *The sun, but a moment before so brilliant, was now almost darkened by smoke and mist enveloping and shadowing the earth, and through which came hissing and shrieking, fiery fuses and messengers of death, sweeping, plunging, cutting, ploughing through our ranks, carrying mutilation, destruction, pain, suffering and death in every direction. Turn your eyes whithersoever you would, and there was to be seen at almost every moment of time, guns, swords, haversacks, human flesh and bones, flying and dangling in the air, or bouncing above the earth...Over us, in front of us, behind us, and in our midst, and through our ranks, poured death on every hand...*[115]

Johnston was struck by a shell fragment in the hip and was unable to participate in the charge.

After two hours, Meade ordered the Union batteries to cease fire. He believed the cannon were doing little harm to the Confederate guns and were simply creating more smoke in the valley.[116] Also, Brigadier General Henry J. Hunt, chief of artillery, wanted to conserve ammunition; therefore, they slowly reduced their fire. In some cases badly damaged cannon were being replaced by new guns from the rear; the Confederates noted cannon being removed but were unaware of their replacements.

Observing the withdrawal of Union cannon, and a decline in their fire, Colonel E. P. Alexander wrote a quick note to Major General Pickett saying, "For God's sake come quick...Come quick or my ammunition will not let me support you properly."[117]

The three Confederate division commanders were Major General George Pickett, Brigadier General J. J. Pettigrew and Major General Isaac Trimble. Eighteen Virginia regiments, fifteen North Carolina regiments, three Mississippi regiments, two Alabama regiments and two Tennessee regiments, a total of 12,500 infantrymen, participated in the attack.[118]

Pickett's division had not been involved in a major engagement since the winter of 1862. His men, therefore, were eager to share in the glory which other units had earned. Pickett was also anxious to command his grand division in the attack. However, he had never before commanded a division in a combat situation. His division attacked the southern end of Cemetery Ridge to the stone wall where it makes a 90° angle. On the other side of the angle, near Bryan's farm and Cemetery Hill, Pettigrew and Trimble's men struck.

The Union infantry in this area numbered around 5,750.[119]

* * * *

Since this charge is well-noted in history, Stop 23 is divided into five parts, and a full account is provided (see map 53).

Go to Stop 23a: Cemetery Ridge, 13th and 16th Vermont Monuments (southern wall), Hancock Avenue.

Map 53

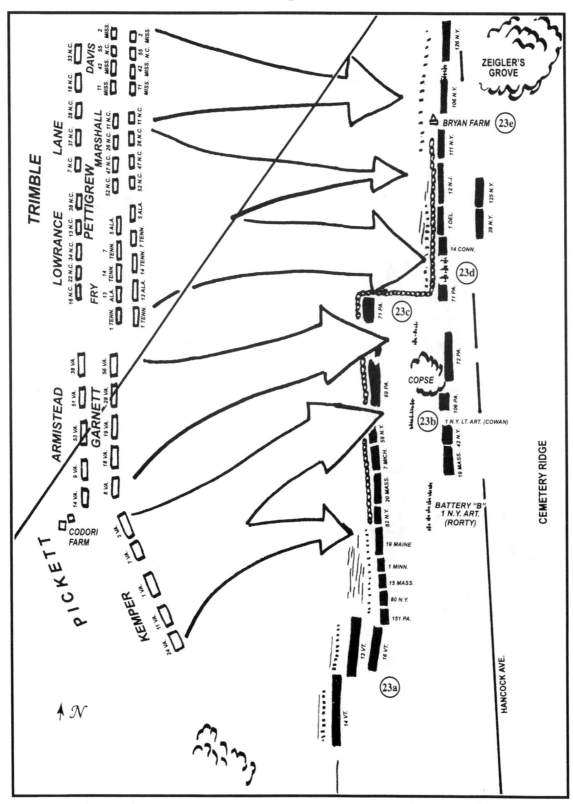

Overview of the final Confederate assault.

Stop 23a: Cemetery Ridge, Vermont Monuments
(Gettysburg National Park Stop 15)

THE FINAL STRUGGLE ON CEMETERY RIDGE

3:00–4:00p.m.

Confederate Division Commander: vs.   **Union Division Commander:**

Major General George Pickett
(4,500 men)

Brigadier General John Gibbon
(3,785 men)*

Confederate Brigade Commander: vs.   **Union Brigade Commanders:**

Brigadier General James Kemper
(1,325 men)

Brigadier General George Stannard
(1,400 men)

---

*This number includes three Vermont regiments and two other Union regiments which were not in Brigadier General Gibbon's division but were stationed on Cemetery Ridge.

Union Brigade Commanders:

Brigadier GeneralWilliam Harrow
(700 men)

Colonel Norman J. Hall
(570 men)

Colonel Francis Voltaire Randall

In this area, up to the copse of trees, approximately 1,325 Confederates fought against 3,215 Union infantrymen.

Upon receiving the message from Alexander, Pickett asked his corps commander, Lieutenant General Longstreet, to move out. Feeling that the attack was ill advised, Longstreet merely bowed his head. Pickett then saluted and said, "I shall lead my division forward, sir."[120] The word passed rapidly to the other Confederate units; the waiting was over.

To the Union soldiers, the huge mass of Confederates resembled a gray ocean tide.[121] When they moved into the open field, the Union cannon on Cemetery Hill, Ridge and Little Round Top fired into the infantrymen. Shot, shell, spherical case, shrapnel and canister, thousands of deadly missiles, raced through the air to thin the Confederate ranks. A projectile exploded in front of a regiment killing three men and wounding five others. "Close up men!" someone shouted, and the gap disappeared as soldiers took the place of the dead and wounded. An officer's head was shattered by a round shot, but his men simply stepped over the body. Again an officer shouted, "Close up!" — "Not too fast on the left" — "Major take command, the Colonel is down," as they continued through the brutal storm of shot and shell.[122] One soldier dropped, announcing he was wounded. When his sergeant demanded to see the wound, the young man ran away. The sergeant followed but lost him in the crowd.[123] The Confederates suffered heavy casualties as they continued their relentless advance across that fateful mile.

After crossing the Emmitsburg road, Brigadier General James Kemper's brigade drifted to the left concentrating on the copse of trees. However, this movement exposed Kemper's right flank. Seizing the opportunity, Brigadier General George Stannard sent against them two Vermont regiments, the 13th and the 16th, who fired a deadly cross-fire into the Confederates and then rushed them with bayonets. They pushed forward, vengefully determined to slay the last man unless they surrendered. Bayonets were crossed and desperate thrusts were exchanged. Many fell wounded and bleeding, pierced with bayonet, sword, and musket balls and bludgeoned with pistols.[124] As the conquered Confederates surrendered, at his own risk Colonel Francis Voltaire Randall, commander of the 13th Vermont, passed rapidly down the front of his regiment shouting, "Stop firing!"[125]

Kemper fell from his horse, shot through the body, the bullet exiting near his groin. He was among those captured by Union troops but was quickly retaken by his own (see map 54).[126]

Hancock was with Stannard when they struck the enemy column. Hancock fell from his horse when he received a serious wound in his thigh. He was carried to a field hospital and survived his wound.[127]

Go to Stop 23b: Cemetery Ridge, Monument of 1st Independent New York Light Artillery Battery, "Cowan's Battery."

Map 54

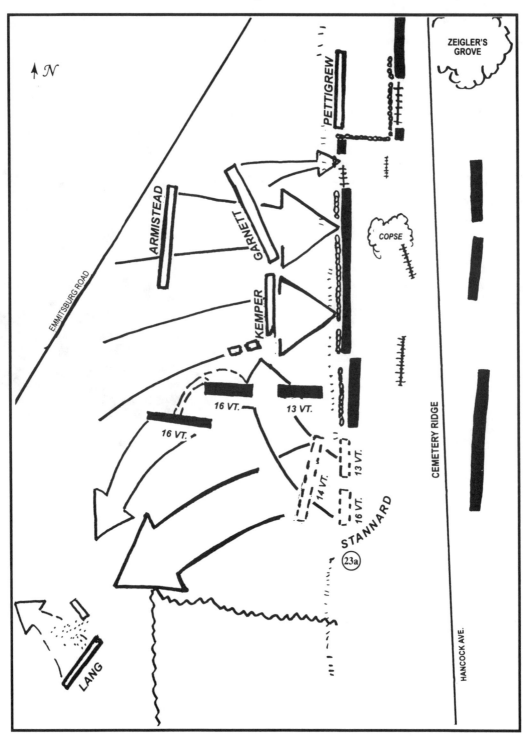

Cemetery Ridge
The 16th Vermont and 13th Vermont fire into Kemper's right flank.
While the 14th Vermont strikes the Confederate reinforcements commanded by Wilcox and Lang.

Stop 23b: Cemetery Ridge, near monument of 1st Independent New York Light Artillery Battery, "Captain Andrew Cowan's Battery"

While Kemper's right flank was being raked by the Vermonters, his left flank breached the wall. To meet them Captain Andrew Cowan's New York battery fired double canister into their midst. Wagon-sized gaps were cut into their line, but more Confederates immediately appeared. Union infantrymen began to break under the pressure. An artillerist from Cowan's battery, impatient and irate with the infantrymen, smashed a coffee pot over one retreating soldier's head. The bottom gave out, and the pot became wrapped around the man's head who, nevertheless, continued his flight.[128]

Surging once again through this small crack, the Virginians met a thunderous roar from Cowan's five cannon, which were spewing out double-shotted canister. When the smoke cleared, not one Confederate remained standing. In some places their mutilated bodies lay three deep (see map 55).[129]

Captain Andrew Cowan

Go to Stop 23c: Cemetery Ridge, "The Angle"

Map 55

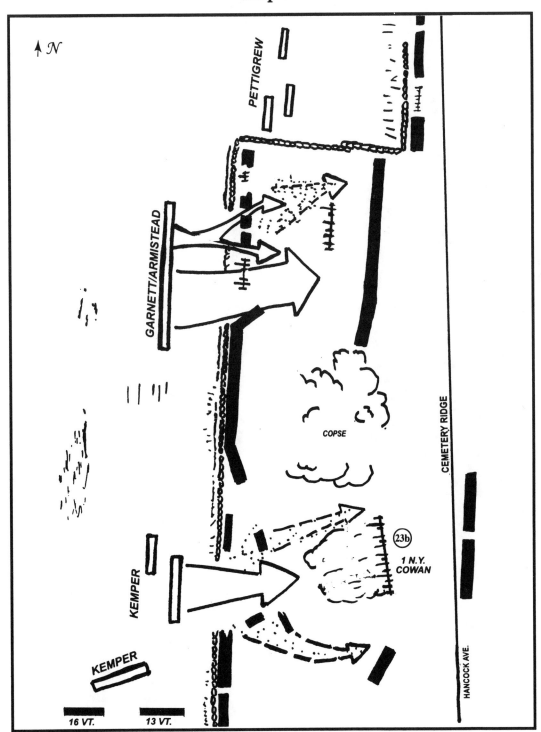

Cemetery Ridge
Captain Cowan's 1st New York battery fires into Kemper's brigade.

Stop 23c: Cemetery Ridge, "The Angle"

Confederate Brigade Commanders: vs.   **Union Brigade Commander:**

Brigadier General Richard B. Garnett
(1,405 men)

Brigadier General Alexander Webb
(880 men)

Brigadier General Lewis Armistead
(1,570 men)

Colonel Dennis O'Kane

Lieutenant Colonel Martin Tschudy

Initially 2,895 Confederates confronted 880 Union soldiers in this area, but the two Confederate brigades suffered heavy casualties while advancing across the open field.

With the entire area engulfed in smoke and deafening noise, the Confederate movement was obscured. Men from the 69th and 71st Pennsylvania soon found Confederate rifles against their chests; the men's clothes were burned from the gun powder. The Confederate musket fire was frightfully effective. Colonel Dennis O'Kane, commander of the 69th Pennsylvania, was shot through the chest; he died on July 5th. A bullet struck Lieutenant Colonel Martin Tschudy in the bladder, killing him. Private William Hayes was shot in the head.[130] Men clubbed one another with their rifles. Under the weight of the attack the two right companies of the 69th refused their line and were now facing northwest. (During July 2 and 3 the 69th lost 122 killed and wounded out of 258 men.)

To the right of the 69th, artillerymen and infantrymen from the 69th and 71st Pennsylvania placed two cannon at the wall. Lieutenant Alonzo Cushing commanded these guns and the other four behind him. Already wounded in the shoulder and groin, he was shot through the mouth; he lay dead next to one of his guns near the wall. [131] With no infantry support, the artillerymen abandoned the guns. Virginians from Brigadier General Richard B. Garnett's and Brigadier General Lewis Armistead's brigades surged through the breach. Garnett had been shot in the head and killed, but Armistead led approximately 200 Confederates over the wall (see map 56). Lieutenant J. Irving Sale, of the 53rd Virginia, Armistead's brigade, described the scene.

It was awful the way the men dropped. When we got right up here a few feet from the stone wall you fellows were behind, we all lay down and blazed away at the top of the wall wherever we could see a head. You blazed back so hard that in about a minute we gave that up and rushed over the wall. General Armistead was right ahead of me...When we poured over the wall, he waved his hat and sword and yelled: 'Now give 'em the cold steel, boys.' Yes, I was only a few feet behind him when he fell...I never saw so many dead men in my life as there were

Lieutenant Alonzo Cushing

here. The blue coats were lying all over so thick that you could scarcely help stepping on them.[132]

Armistead jumped the wall and started toward the second Union line. With his hat on the tip of his sword he yelled, "Come on boys, give them cold steel! Who will follow me?" Nearing the four abandoned cannon he fell shot in the leg and arm.

Union troops, who had scattered at the wall, were reformed. Officers in this area drew their swords and yelled, "halt," "face about" and, "fire." Those soldiers who did not quickly obey were slapped with the flat of the sabre. Assimilated into the second line, twelve Union regiments from Pennsylvania, Maine, Massachusetts, Michigan, Minnesota, and New York fired at the onrushing Virginians.[133] The two lines collided; man-to-man, foot-to-foot, body-to-body they pushed and struggled to win ground. The wounded were everywhere; the bodies of the dead entangled the feet of the contestants. Soldiers fought hatless and coatless covered with sweat and black powder and red with blood. One could hear fiendish yells and swearing as men blindly struck one another.[134] After a short melée, the sorely outnumbered Confederates either retreated or surrendered.

* * * *

Lewis Armistead died July 5 at the age of forty-six. His last words to a Union surgeon were, "Men who can subsist on raw corn, can never be whipped."[135]

Go to Stop 23d: Cemetery Ridge, Cannon of Battery A, 1st Rhode Island Light Artillery

Map 56

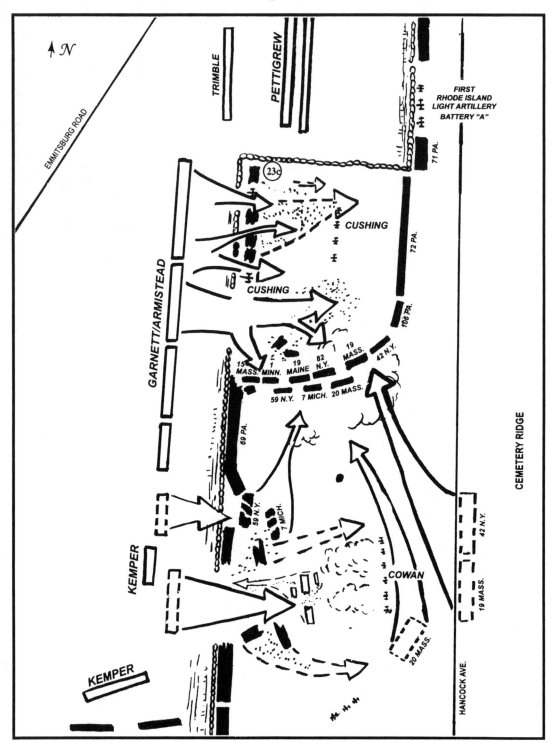

Cemetery Ridge
Armistead's brigade breaks through the Union line at the angle.

Stop 23d: Cemetery Ridge, Cannon of Battery A, 1st Rhode Island Light Artillery

Confederate Division Commanders: vs.   **Union Division Commander:**

*Brigadier General J. J. Pettigrew

Brigadier General Alexander Hays
(1,920 men)

**Major General Isaac Trimble
(5,600 men)

* His hand was struck by canister.
** Near Emmitsburg Road Major General Trimble was wounded in the left leg by a bullet. He survived his injury but was later captured.

Confederate Brigade Commanders: vs.   **Union Brigade Commanders:**

Colonel Birkett D. Fry
(900 men)

Colonel Thomas Smyth
(830 men)

Brigadier General J. J. Pettigrew
(1500 men)

Colonel Eliakim Sherrill
(930 men)

Brigadier General Joseph Davis

During the cannonade, Colonel Fry was hit in the shoulder from a shell fragment. He stayed with his command. Colonel James K. Marshall assumed command of Pettigrew's brigade when Pettigrew received a field promotion to Heth's division. Marshall, shot through the body, fell dead from his horse. Colonel Sherrill was shot in the abdomen and killed during the attack on July 3.

Confederate Brigade Commanders:

**Brigadier General James Lane
(1200 men)**

***Brigadier General A. M. Scales
(500 men)**

*Leading Scales' brigade during the charge was Colonel William Lee J. Lowrance of the 34th North Carolina regiment.

Although the Confederates initially outnumbered the Union troops in this area, they suffered heavily during their advance.

To the right of the angle, near the wall, Battery A of the 1st Rhode Island Light Artillery, fired double-shotted canister into the charging North Carolinians. One of the Union gunners waited until the Confederates were at the wall. Then Sergeant Amos M. C. Olney cried out, "Barker, why the [damn] don't you fire that [cannon]! pull! pull!"[136] The gap made in Fry's and Lowrance's regiments was incomprehensible (see map 57).

Sergeant Amos Olney

Go to Stop 23e: Cemetery Ridge, Bryan's Farm.

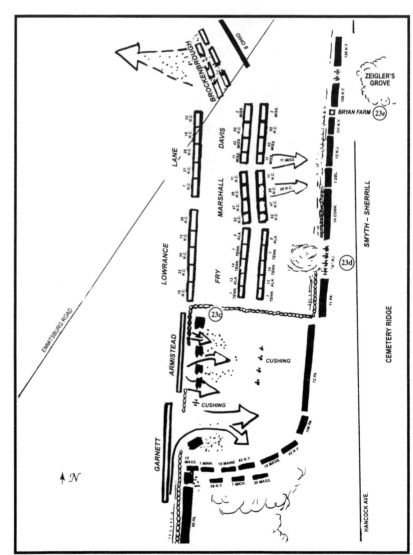

Map 57
Cemetery Ridge
Battery "A," 1st Rhode Island,
Light Artillery fires into Fry's and
Lowrance's brigade.

Stop 23e: Cemetery Ridge, Bryan's Farm

While the Vermont regiments struck Kemper's right flank, Union troops to the far right hit the Confederate left flank.

Lieutenant Colonel Franklin Sawyer's 8th Ohio, deployed near the Emmitsburg road, charged Colonel J. M. Brockenbrough's brigade. Many Confederates were killed or captured. The remaining men fell back to Seminary Ridge. With Brockenbrough's brigade gone, the 8th Ohio faced left. Near Bryan's farm, the 126th New York regiment, and two Napoleon cannon, swung left to join the 8th Ohio. The two regiments and cannon sent a deadly enfilading fire into the Confederate flank. Davis's and Marshall's Confederate line disappeared. Smoke engulfed the area and only small, unorganized clusters of Confederate soldiers were left to continue the charge. Captain S. P. Wagg of the 26th North Carolina fell dead, shot through with shrapnel.[137] Lieutenant George Woodruff, commander of the two Union cannon, was also mortally wounded.

Lieutenant Colonel Franklin Sawyer

Captain S. P. Wagg

Lieutenant George Woodruff

The 12th New Jersey infantrymen noted a "smooth-cheeked lad,...the leader of thousands, [run]...forward through all that fire to fall dead... covered with wounds within twenty feet of [the Union] colors."[138]

One of those smooth-cheeked boys was Private Thomas F. McKie of the 11th Mississippi, "University Greys." He was only sixteen years old when he enlisted in March of 1862. He fought in thirteen engagements; nevertheless, Tommie, like all of the soldiers, yearned to go home. Several months before the battle of Gettysburg, Thomas wrote to his mother asking that she write President Jefferson Davis to get "him off." His mother, however, was unable to arrange this. On Friday afternoon, July 3, as he marched toward Bryan's farm, the young man was mortally wounded in the stomach and later died in a Union hospital.[139]

Soldiers from the 55th North Carolina and 11th Mississippi fought from behind Bryan's farm. A Mississippi lieutenant fell within ten feet of the Union line. Struck from the front and sides, and with continuous cannon fire from Cemetery Hill and Little Round Top, the Confederate tide ebbed (see map 58).[140]

Division commanders Pettigrew and Trimble had led closely behind their men, both receiving wounds. Pickett and his staff supervised his division near the Codori Farm.[141] As Pickett rode back to Seminary Ridge, Lee stopped him and said, "General Pickett, place your division in [the] rear of this hill, and be ready to repel the advance of the enemy should they follow up their advantage."[142]

Pickett merely bowed his head and said, "General Lee, I have no division now. Armistead is down, Garnett is down, and Kemper is mortally wounded."[143] (Kemper survived.)

Lee answered, "Come, General Pickett, this has been my fight, and upon my shoulders rests the blame. The men and officers of your command have written the name of Virginia as high today as it has ever been written before."[144]

Private Thomas McKie

Pickett took into battle nearly 4,500 men; 500 were killed, 2,007 were wounded and 375 were captured, a total of 2,882 Virginians, 67 percent. Pettigrew's division lost 470 killed, 1,893 wounded, 337 were captured, a total of 2,700, 60 percent. It was the 26th North Carolina that had suffered heavily against the Iron Brigade on the first day of fighting. After the third day, they had only 80 men, out of 800, to report for duty. Trimble's force suffered 155 killed, 650 wounded, 80 men were captured, a total of 885, 52 percent. In just one hour, the entire Confederate loss, including prisoners, was 7,500 men. The Union suffered 1,500 losses, a ratio of five-to-one.[145]

Between Seminary Ridge and Cemetery Ridge there lay at least 7,175 soldiers dead and wounded (5,675 Confederates, 1,500 Union). Two of these ca-

Map 58

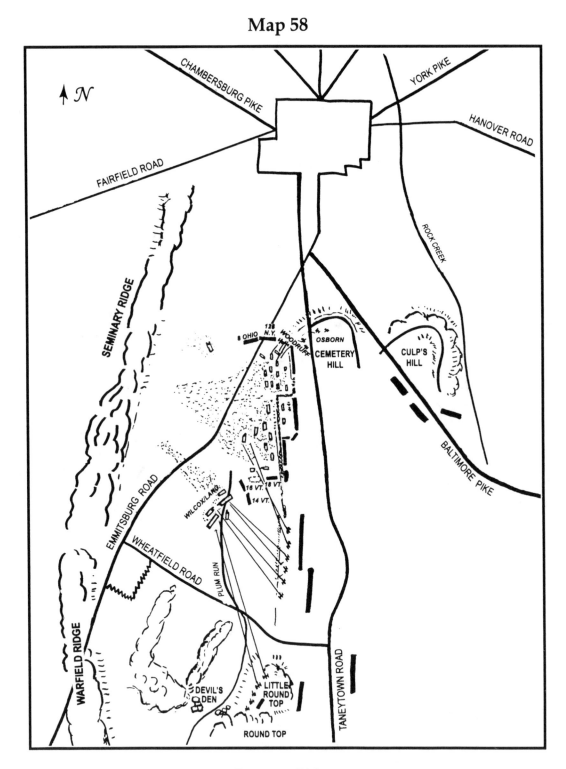

Cemetery Ridge
"Double-Envelope"

On the Union right the 8th Ohio, 126th New York and two cannon fire into the Confederate left flank. At the center, Union regiments are rushed in and on the Union left Stannard's Vermont regiments strike the Confederate right flank.

sualties were women. One Confederate woman was found dead on the field and another was wounded. She was taken to a Union field hospital where doctors amputated her leg. No names were revealed.[146] Lee took full responsibility for the failed attack (see map 59).

Map 59

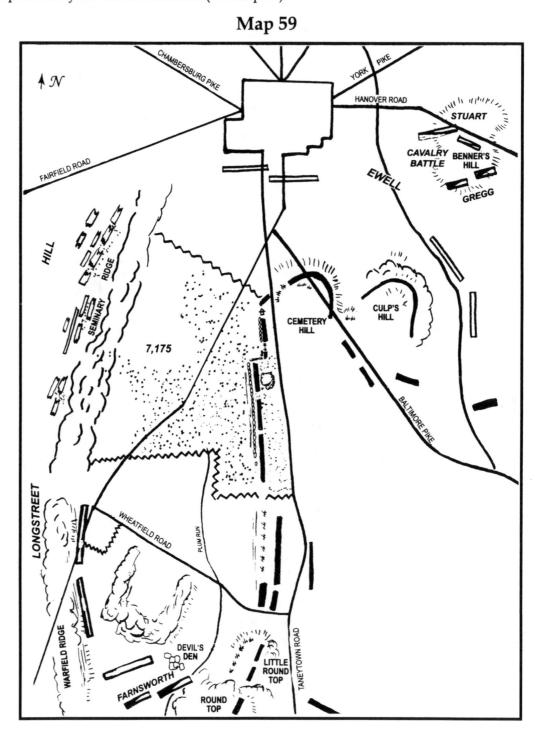

Cemetery Ridge

Over 7,000 soldiers fell during the final assault on July 3. Around 3:00 p.m. July 3, near the Hanover road, the cavalry battle occurred and near Big Round Top, at 5:00 p.m., General Farnsworth makes his fatal charge.

CAVALRY BATTLES

July 3

Confederate Commanders: vs. Union Commanders:

Major General Jeb Stuart

Brigadier General David Gregg

As part of Lee's grand strategy for July 3rd he ordered Stuart's cavalry force (6,000 men) to ride around the right flank of the Union army and cause havoc in their rear. This expedition, however, was interrupted by Brigadier General David Gregg's and Brigadier General George Custer's cavalry forces (5,000 men). The battle took place around 3:00 p.m., two-and-a-half miles east of Gettysburg on the Hanover Road, while Pickett's Charge was taking place minutes away. There were mounted charges and counter-charges. After a vicious hand-to-hand melée the Union troops drove the Confederates from the field. One of the Confederate brigades had only ten rounds of ammunition and Stuart, therefore, was forced to retreat (see map 59).[147]

Brigadier General George Armstrong Custer

The last struggle at Gettysburg occurred near the Big Round Top/Devil's Den area. Around 5:30 p.m., Brigadier General Elon J. Farnsworth's cavalry brigade was ordered to make a mounted charge on the Confederate right flank. Farnsworth protested strongly, stating it was suicide; however, he obeyed his orders and led his Union cavalry into the Confederate infantry. The result was a disaster. The cavalrymen presented perfect targets and were shot down. Farnsworth's brigade was cut to pieces, and the general was killed, shot five times.

Ironically, the Battle of Gettysburg opened and closed with Union cavalry fighting Confederate infantry.

Brigadier General Elon J. Farnsworth

SUMMARY OF FRIDAY, JULY 3

General Lee once again proposed a three-pronged attack; the main thrust was directed at the Union center. However, due to lack of communication, or poor generalship, the Confederates on the left attacked early in the morning not waiting for a simultaneous effort. After five and a half hours of fighting (6:30-11:30 a.m.) the Confederates were compelled to retreat from Culp's Hill. At 1:00 p.m. the battle recommenced with a magnificent two hour artillery duel. Then, at 3:00 p.m., 12,500 Confederates crossed a mile-wide field and charged the Union line on Cemetery Ridge. For an hour the battle raged, but the Confederates, exhausted and overwhelmed by numbers, were forced to retreat back to Seminary Ridge.

During the afternoon two cavalry battles took place. On the far Union right the Confederates were defeated. On the far Union left the cavalry were repulsed by Confederate infantrymen.

Casualties:

The Union army suffered 3,858 killed or wounded. The Confederates lost 6,326 killed or wounded. Overall 10,184 Americans were killed or wounded on July 3, 1863.

The Battle of Gettysburg came to a devastating conclusion. The Confederate army halted; both sides had suffered heavy casualties.

	Union	Confederate
Killed	3,155	3,903
Wounded*	14,529	18,735
Missing	5,365	5,425

The Union counted 17,684 killed and wounded; Confederate killed and wounded numbered 22,638, a total of 40,322 men in just three days.[148]

To understand the enormous three-day casualty rate one might compare the numbers from the American Revolution, the War of 1812, and the Mexican War added together.

	Americans Killed and Wounded
American Revolution, 1775-1781.	10,623
War of 1812, 1812-1815.	6,765
Mexican War, 1846-1848.	17,435

11-year total: 34,823

Gettysburg, July 1, 2, 3, 1863, total: 40,322

*Includes mortally wounded and captured. Missing could include lost, killed, captured or deserted. The National Park averages there were 51,000 total casualties.

Conclusion

SATURDAY, JULY 4

In July of 1863 the small town of Gettysburg, with about 2,400 citizens, found itself invaded by 160,000 soldiers. For three days the two armies fought in the surrounding fields, woods, hills and orchards. After the battle, the Confederates began the long retreat to Virginia, leaving most of their wounded and dead behind. The Union army followed, with the exception of those soldiers on burial detail. The overwhelming number of wounded, however, were cared for by local citizens, the Union medical corps and other civilians who came from all parts of the North with offers of aid.

On July 4 it began to rain, and the blood was washed from those fields on which the soldiers had fought and died.

The Battle of Gettysburg signified the Confederate high tide; no other campaign reached this far North. They had hoped to achieve a great victory in Northern territory and finish the war. Instead, the Southerners were driven from Union soil. Moreover, their sense of invincibility was toppled, and their morale was low. Coupled with the defeat at Vicksburg, Mississippi the same day, the Confederate States of America had suffered a devastating blow.

The Union army, on the other hand, achieved a great victory and gained a sense of confidence, in itself and in its generals, which had been sorely lacking. This new-found assurance aided the Union in carrying through with the remaining campaigns of the Civil War.

The Battle of Gettysburg was also the bloodiest battle in U.S. history and is the most widely recognized Civil War conflict. For more than 130 years, monuments, donated by veterans and individual states, have been dedicated throughout the Park to honor the individuals who fought and died here. Consequently, Gettysburg is one of the best marked battlefields in the world and one of the most visited. In addition, it has been the subject of thousands of books, articles and hundreds of speeches. Nevertheless, no author has succeeded more than Abraham Lincoln, in his "Gettysburg Address," in placing Gettysburg in the hearts of the people. In a mere two minutes, the President immortalized the battlefield as a hallmark for the continuing struggle for freedom and its high cost to those living and dead.

Go to Stop 24: Cemetery Hill, National Cemetery, Lincoln's Memorial

Stop 24: National Cemetery, Soldiers' National Monument
(Gettysburg National Park Stop 16)

THURSDAY, NOVEMBER 19, 1863

Ceremonies were held for the purpose of dedicating Cemetery Hill as a National Cemetery. One of the speakers on that day was President Abraham Lincoln. In his abbreviated address he stated:

Four score and seven years ago our fathers brought forth, upon this continent, a new nation, conceived in Liberty, and dedicated to the proposition that all men are created equal.

Now we are engaged in a great civil war, testing whether that nation, or any nation, so conceived, and so dedicated, can long endure. We are met here on a great battlefield of that war. We have come to dedicate a portion of it as a final resting place for those who gave their lives that that nation might live. It is altogether fitting and proper that we should do this.

But in a larger sense we can not dedicate — we can not consecrate — we can not hallow — this ground. The brave men, living and dead, who struggled here, have consecrated it, far above our poor power to add or detract. The world will little note, nor long remember, what we say here, but can never forget what they did here. It is for us, the living, rather to be dedicated here to the unfinished work which they have, thus far, so nobly carried on. It is rather for us to be here dedicated to the great task remaining before us — that from these honored dead we take increased devotion to that cause for which they gave the last full measure of devotion — that we here highly resolve that these dead shall not have died in vain; that this nation shall have a new birth of freedom; and that this government of the people, by the people, and for the people shall not perish from the earth.

* * * *

The President was mistaken about one thing; the world has not forgotten, not only the deeds carried out here, but his words which turned the Battle of Gettysburg into a symbol of the war for the Union. It was for this, as much as for its oratorical merits, that his speech is remembered.[149]

Appendix A

The Civil War ended on April 9, 1865, nearly two years after the great Battle of Gettysburg.

The total deaths for both sides in the War is placed conservatively at 623,026. Total American deaths in wars following: World War I - 116,708; World War II - 407,316; Korean War - 54,246 — a total of 591,853, a number short of those killed in the Civil War alone.[150]

Official Rosters

(Corps and division commanders are listed in the order that they assumed command.)

UNITS OF THE ARMY OF THE POTOMAC, U.S.A., AT THE BATTLE OF GETTYSBURG, JULY 1-3, 1863

Major General George G. Meade, commanding

ARMY HEADQUARTERS

Maj. Gen. Daniel Butterfield, chief of staff
Brig. Gen. G. K. Warren, chief of engineers
Brig. Gen. Henry J. Hunt, chief of artillery
Brig. Gen. Marsena R. Patrick, provost marshall general
Brig. Gen. Seth Williams, assistant adjutant general
Brig. Gen. Rufus Ingalls, chief quartermaster
Dr. Jonathan Letterman, medical director
Capt. Lemuel B. Norton, chief signal officer
Lt. John R. Edie, acting chief ordnance officer

COMMAND OF THE PROVOST MARSHAL GENERAL

2nd Pennsylvania Cavalry
6th Pennsylvania Cavalry, Companies E and I
Regular cavalry (detachments from 1st, 2nd, 5th, and 6th Regiments)

I CORPS

Maj. Gen. John F. Reynolds
Maj. Gen. Abner Doubleday
Maj. Gen. John Newton

GENERAL HEADQUARTERS

1st Maine Cavalry, Company L

FIRST DIVISION
Brig. Gen. James S. Wadsworth

1st Brigade

Brig. Gen. Solomon Meredith
Col. William W. Robinson

19th Indiana
24th Michigan
2nd Wisconsin
6th Wisconsin
7th Wisconsin

2nd Brigade

Brig. Gen. Lysander Cutler

7th Indiana
76th New York
84th New York (14th Militia)
95th New York
147th New York
56th Pennsylvania (nine companies)

SECOND DIVISION
Brig. Gen. John C. Robinson

1st Brigade

Brig. Gen. Gabriel R. Paul
Col. Samuel H. Leonard
Col. Adrian R. Root
Col. Richard Coulter
Col. Peter Lyle
Col. Richard Coulter

16th Maine
13th Massachusetts
94th New York
104th New York
107th Pennsylvania

2nd Brigade

Brig. Gen. Henry Baxter

12th Massachusetts
83rd New York (9th Militia)
97th New York
11th Pennsylvania
88th Pennsylvania
90th Pennsylvania

THIRD DIVISION
Brig. Gen. Thomas A. Rowley
Maj. Gen. Abner Doubleday

1st Brigade

Col. Chapman Biddle
Brig. Gen. Thomas A. Rowley
Col. Chapman Biddle

80th New York (20th Militia)
121st Pennsylvania
142nd Pennsylvania
151st Pennsylvania

2nd Brigade

Col. Roy Stone
Col. Langhorne Wister
Col. Edmund L. Dana

143rd Pennsylvania
149th Pennsylvania
150th Pennsylvania

3rd Brigade

Brig. Gen. George J. Stannard
Col. Francis V. Randall

13th Vermont
14th Vermont
16th Vermont

Artillery Brigade
Col. Charles S. Wainwright
Maine Light, 2nd Battery (B)
Maine Light, 5th Battery (E)
1st New York Light, Battery L and E
1st Pennsylvania Light, Battery B
4th United States, Battery B

II CORPS
Maj. Gen. Winfield S. Hancock
Brig. Gen. John Gibbon
Maj. Gen. Winfield S. Hancock

GENERAL HEADQUARTERS
6th New York Cavalry, Companies D and K

FIRST DIVISION
Brig. Gen. John C. Caldwell

1st Brigade
Col. Edward E. Cross
Col. H. Boyd McKeen

5th New Hampshire
61st New York
81st Pennsylvania
148th Pennsylvania

2nd Brigade
Col. Patrick Kelly

28th Massachusetts
63rd New York (two companies)
69th New York (two companies)
88th New York (two companies)
116th Pennsylvania (four companies)

3rd Brigade
Brig. Gen. Samuel K. Zook
Lt. Col. John Fraser

52nd New York
57th New York
66th New York
140th Pennsylvania

4th Brigade
Col. John R. Brooke

27th Connecticut (two companies)
2nd Delaware
64th New York
53rd Pennsylvania
145th Pennsylvania (seven companies)

SECOND DIVISION
Brig. Gen. John Gibbon
Brig. Gen. William Harrow
Brig. Gen. John Gibbon

1st Brigade
Brig. Gen. William Harrow
Col. Francis E. Heath

19th Maine
15th Massachusetts
1st Minnesota and 2d Company
    Minnesota Sharpshooters
82nd New York (2d Militia)

2nd Brigade
Brig. Gen. Alexander S. Webb

69th Pennsylvania
71st Pennsylvania
72nd Pennsylvania
106th Pennsylvania

3rd Brigade
Col. Norman J. Hall

19th Massachusetts
20th Massachusetts
7th Michigan
42nd New York
59th New York (four companies)

Unattached

Massachusetts Sharpshooters,
1st Company

THIRD DIVISION
Brig. Gen. Alexander Hays

1st Brigade
Col. Samuel S. Carroll

14th Indiana
4th Ohio
8th Ohio
7th West Virginia

2nd Brigade
Col. Thomas A. Smyth
Lt. Col. Francis E. Pierce

14th Connecticut
1st Delaware
12th New Jersey
10th New York (battalion)
108th New York

3rd Brigade
Col. George L. Willard
Col. Eliakim Sherrill
Lt. Col. James M. Bull

39th New York (four companies)
111th New York
125th New York
126th New York

Artillery Brigade
Capt. John G. Hazard

1st New York Light, Battery B and 14th New York Battery
1st Rhode Island Light, Battery A
1st Rhode Island Light, Battery B
1st United States, Battery I
4th United States, Battery A

III CORPS
Maj. Gen. Daniel E. Sickles
Maj. Gen. David B. Birney

FIRST DIVISION
Maj. Gen. David B. Birney
Brig. Gen. J. H. Hobart Ward

1st Brigade

Brig. Gen. Charles K. Graham
Col. Andrew H. Tippin

57th Pennsylvania (eight companies)
63rd Pennsylvania
68th Pennsylvania
105th Pennsylvania
114th Pennsylvania
141st Pennsylvania

2nd Brigade

Brig. Gen. J. H. Hobart Ward
Col. Hiram Berdan

20th Indiana
3rd Maine
4th Maine
86th New York
124th New York
99th Pennsylvania
1st United States Sharpshooters
2nd United States Sharpshooters
(eight companies)

3rd Brigade

Col. P. Regis De Trobriand

17th Maine
3rd Michigan
5th Michigan
40th New York
110th Pennsylvania (six companies)

SECOND DIVISION

Brig. Gen. Andrew A. Humphreys

1st Brigade

Brig. Gen. Joseph B. Carr

1st Massachusetts
11th Massachusetts
16th Massachusetts
12th New Hampshire
11th New Jersey
26th Pennsylvania

2nd Brigade

Col. William R. Brewster

70th New York
71st New York
72nd New York
73rd New York
74th New York
120th New York

3rd Brigade

Col. George C. Burling

2nd New Hampshire
5th New Jersey
6th New Jersey
7th New Jersey
8th New Jersey
115th Pennsylvania

Artillery Brigade
Capt. George E. Randolph
Capt. A. Judson Clark

New Jersey Light, 2nd Battery
1st New York Light, Battery D
New York Light, 4th Battery
1st Rhode Island Light, Battery E
4th United States, Battery K

V CORPS
Maj. Gen. George Sykes

GENERAL HEADQUARTERS
12th New York Infantry, Companies D and E
17th Pennsylvania Cavalry, Companies D and H

FIRST DIVISION
Brig. Gen. James Barnes

1st Brigade
Col. William S. Tilton

18th Massachusetts
22nd Massachusetts
1st Michigan
118th Pennsylvania

2nd Brigade
Col. Jacob B. Sweitzer

9th Massachusetts
32nd Massachusetts
4th Michigan
62nd Pennsylvania

3rd Brigade
Col. Strong Vincent
Col. James C. Rice

20th Maine
16th Michigan
44th New York
83rd Pennsylvania

SECOND DIVISION
Brig. Gen. Romeyn B. Ayres

1st Brigade
Col. Hannibal Day

3rd United States (six companies)
4th United States (four companies)
6th United States (five companies)
12th United States (eight companies)
14th United States (eight companies)

2nd Brigade
Col. Sidney Burbank

2nd United States (six companies)
7th United States (four companies)
10th United States (three companies)
11th United States (six companies)
17th United States (seven companies)

3rd Brigade
Brig. Gen. Stephen H. Weed
Col. Kenner Garrard

140th New York
146th New York
91st Pennsylvania
155th Pennsylvania

THIRD DIVISION
Brig. Gen. Samuel W. Crawford

1st Brigade
Col. William McCandless

1st Pennsylvania Reserves (nine companies)
2nd Pennsylvania Reserves
6th Pennsylvania Reserves
13th Pennsylvania Reserves

3rd Brigade
Col. Joseph W. Fisher

5th Pennsylvania Reserves
9th Pennsylvania Reserves
10th Pennsylvania Reserves
11th Pennsylvania Reserves
12th Pennsylvania Reserves (nine compnaies)

Artillery Brigade
Capt. Augustus P. Martin

Massachusetts Light, 3rd Battery (C)
1st New York Light, Battery C
1st Ohio Light, Battery L
5th United States, Battery D
5th United States, Battery I

VI CORPS
Maj. Gen. John Sedgwick

GENERAL HEADQUARTERS
1st New Jersey Cavalry, Company L
1st Pennsylvania Cavalry, Company H

FIRST DIVISION
Brig. Gen. Horatio G. Wright

PROVOST GUARD
4th New Jersey (three companies)

1st Brigade
Brig. Gen. A. T. A. Torbert

1st New Jersey
2nd New Jersey
3rd New Jersey
15th New Jersey

2nd Brigade
Brig. Gen. Joseph J. Bartlett

5th Maine
121st New York
95th Pennsylvania
96th Pennsylvania

3rd Brigade
Brig. Gen. David A. Russell

6th Maine
49th Pennsylvania (four companies)
119th Pennsylvania
5th Wisconsin

SECOND DIVISION
Brig. Gen. Albion P. Howe

2nd Brigade
Col. Lewis A. Grant

2nd Vermont
3rd Vermont
4th Vermont
5th Vermont
6th Vermont

3rd Brigade
Brig. Gen. Thomas H. Neill

7th Maine (six companies)
33rd New York (detachment)
43rd New York
49th New York
77th New York
61st Pennsylvania

THIRD DIVISION
Maj. Gen. John Newton
Brig. Gen. Frank Wheaton

1st Brigade
Brig. Gen. Alexander Shaler

65th New York
67th New York
122nd New York
23rd Pennsylvania
82nd Pennsylvania

2nd Brigade
Col. Henry L. Eustis

7th Massachusetts
10th Massachusetts
37th Massachusetts
2nd Rhode Island

3rd Brigade
Brig. Gen. Frank Wheaton
Col. David J. Nevin

62nd New York
93rd Pennsylvania
98th Pennsylvania
139th Pennsylvania

Artillery Brigade
Col. Charles H. Tompkins

Massachusetts Light, 1st Battery (A)
New York Light, 1st Battery
New York Light, 3rd Battery
1st Rhode Island Light, Battery C
1st Rhode Island Light, Battery G
2nd United States, Battery D
2nd United States, Battery G
5th United States, Battery F

XI CORPS
Maj. Gen. Oliver O. Howard
Maj. Gen. Carl Schurz
Maj. Gen. Oliver O. Howard

GENERAL HEADQUARTERS
1st Indiana Cavalry, Companies I and K
8th New York Infantry (one company)

FIRST DIVISION
Brig. Gen. Francis C. Barlow
Brig. Gen. Adelbert Ames

1st Brigade	*2nd Brigade*
Col. Leopold Von Gilsa	Brig. Gen. Adelbert Ames
	Col. Andrew L. Harris
41st New York (nine companies)	17th Connecticut
54th New York	25th Ohio
68th New York	75th Ohio
153rd Pennsylvania	107th Ohio

SECOND DIVISION
Brig. Gen. Adolph Von Steinwehr

1st Brigade	*2nd Brigade*
Col. Charles R. Coster	Col. Orland Smith
134th New York	33rd Massachusetts
154th New York	136th New York
27th Pennsylvania	55th Ohio
73rd Pennsylvania	73rd Ohio

THIRD DIVISION

Maj. Gen. Carl Schurz
Brig. Gen. Alex. Schimmelfennig
Maj. Gen. Carl Schurz

1st Brigade

Brig. Gen. Alex. Schimmelfennig
Col. George Von Amsberg

82nd Illinois
45th New York
157th New York
61st Ohio
74th Pennsylvania

2nd Brigade

Col. W. Krzyzanowski

58th New York
119th New York
82nd Ohio
75th Pennsylvania
26th Wisconsin

Artillery Brigade

Maj. Thomas W. Osborn

1st New York Light, Battery I
New York Light, 13th Battery
1st Ohio Light, Battery I
1st Ohio Light, Battery K
4th United States, Battery G

XII CORPS

Maj. Gen. Henry W. Slocum
Brig. Gen. Alpheus S. Williams

PROVOST GUARD

10th Maine (four companies)

FIRST DIVISION

Brig. Gen. Alpheus S. Williams
Brig. Gen. Thomas H. Ruger

1st Brigade

Col. Archibald L. McDougall

5th Connecticut
20th Connecticut
3rd Maryland
123rd New York
145th New York
46th Pennsylvania

2nd Brigade

Brig. Gen. Henry H. Lockwood

1st Maryland, Potomac Home Brigade
1st Maryland, Eastern Shore
150th New York

3rd Brigade

Brig. Gen. Thomas H. Ruger
Col. Silas Colgrove

27th Indiana
2nd Massachusetts
13th New Jersey
107th New York
3rd Wisconsin

SECOND DIVISION

Brig. Gen. John W. Geary

1st Brigade

Col. Charles Candy

5th Ohio
7th Ohio
29th Ohio
66th Ohio
28th Pennsylvania
147th Pennsylvania (eight companies)

2nd Brigade

Col. George A. Cobham, Jr.
Brig. Gen. Thomas L. Kane
Col. George A. Cobham, Jr.

29th Pennsylvania
109th Pennsylvania
111th Pennsylvania

3rd Brigade

Brig. Gen. George S. Greene

60th New York
78th New York
102nd New York
137th New York
149th New York

Artillery Brigade

Lt. Edward D. Muhlenberg

1st New York Light, Battery M
Pennsylvania Light, Battery E
4th United States, Battery F
5th United States, Battery K

CAVALRY CORPS

Maj. Gen. Alfred Pleasonton

FIRST DIVISION
Brig. Gen. John Buford

1st Brigade
Col. William Gamble

8th Illinois
12th Illinois
3rd Indiana (six companies)
8th New York

2nd Brigade
Col. Thomas C. Devin

6th New York
9th New York
17th Pennsylvania
3rd West Virginia (two companies)

Reserve Brigade
Brig. Gen. Wesley Merritt

6th Pennsylvania
1st United States
2nd United States
5th United States
6th United States

SECOND DIVISION
Brig. Gen. David McM. Gregg

Headquarters Guard
1st Ohio, Company A

1st Brigade
Col. John B. McIntosh

1st Maryland (eleven companies)
Purnell (Maryland) Legion, Company A
1st Massachusetts
1st New Jersey
1st Pennsylvania
3rd Pennsylvania
3rd Pennsylvania Artillery, Section

3rd Brigade
Col. J. Irvin Gregg

1st Maine (ten companies)
10th New York
4th Pennsylvania
16th Pennsylvania

THIRD DIVISION
Brig. Gen. Judson Kilpatrick

Headquarters Guard
1st Ohio, Company C

1st Brigade
Brig. Gen. Elon J. Farnsworth
Col. Nathaniel P. Richmond

2nd Brigade
Brig. Gen. George A. Custer

5th New York
18th Pennsylvania
1st Vermont
1st West Virginia

1st Michigan
5th Michigan
6th Michigan
7th Michigan (ten companies)

HORSE ARTILLERY

1st Brigade
Capt. James M. Robertson

9th Michigan Battery
6th New York Battery
2nd United States, Batteries B and L
2nd United States, Battery M
4th United States, Battery E

2nd Brigade
Capt. John C. Tidball

1st United States, Batteries E and G
1st United States, Battery K
2nd United States, Battery A

ARTILLERY RESERVE
Brig. Gen. Robert O. Tyler
Capt. James M. Robertson

Headquarters Guard
32nd Massachusetts Infantry, Company C

1st Regular Brigade
Capt. Dunbar R. Ransom

1st United States, Battery H
3rd United States, Batteries F and K
4th United States, Battery C
5th United States, Battery C

1st Volunteer Brigade
Lt. Col. Freeman McGilvery

Massachusetts Light, 5th Battery (E)
  and 10th New York Battery
Massachusetts Light, 9th Battery
New York Light, 15th Battery
Pennsylvania Light, Batteries C and F

2nd Volunteer Brigade
Capt. Elijah D. Taft

Connecticut Light, 2nd Battery
New York Light, 5th Battery

3rd Volunteer Brigade
Capt. James F. Huntington

New Hampshire Light, 1st Battery
1st Ohio Light, Battery H
1st Pennsylvania Light, Batteries F and G
West Virginia Light, Battery C

4th Volunteer Brigade
Capt. Robert H. Fitzhugh

Maine Light, 6th Battery (F)
Maryland Light, Battery A
New Jersey Light, 1st Battery
1st New York Light, Battery G
1st New York Light, Battery K and 11th New York Battery

Train Guard
4th New Jersey Infantry (seven companies)

UNITS OF THE ARMY OF NORTHERN VIRGINIA, C.S.A., AT THE BATTLE OF GETTYSBURG, JULY 1-3, 1863

General Robert E. Lee, commanding

ARMY HEADQUARTERS

Col. R. H. Chilton, chief of staff and inspector general
Brig. Gen. W. N. Pendleton, chief of artillery
Dr. Lafayette Guild, medical director
Lt. Col. Briscoe G. Baldwin, chief of ordnance
Lt. Col. Robert G. Cole, chief of commissary
Lt. Col. James L. Corley, chief quartermaster
Maj. H. E. Young, judge advocate general
Col. A. L. Long, military secretary and acting assistant chief of artillery
Lt. Col. Walter H. Taylor, aide de camp and assistant adjutant general
Maj. Charles Marshall, aide de camp and assistant military secretary
Maj. Charles S. Venable, aide de camp and assistant inspector general
Capt. S. R. Johnston, engineer

I CORPS
Lt. Gen. James Longstreet

McLAWS' DIVISION
Maj. Gen. Lafayette McLaws

Kershaw's Brigade
Brig. Gen. J. B. Kershaw

2nd South Carolina
3rd South Carolina
7th South Carolina
8th South Carolina
15th South Carolina
3rd South Carolina Battalion

Semmes' Brigade
Brig. Gen. P. J. Semmes
Col. Goode Bryan

10th Georgia
50th Georgia
51st Georgia
53rd Georgia

Barksdale's Brigade
Brig. Gen. William Barksdale
Col. B. G. Humphreys

13th Mississippi
17th Mississippi
18th Mississippi
21st Mississippi

Wofford's Brigade
Brig. Gen. W. T. Wofford

16th Georgia
18th Georgia
24th Georgia
Cobb's (Georgia) Legion
Phillips (Georgia) Legion

Artillery
Col. H. C. Cabell

1st North Carolina Artillery, Battery A
Pulaski (Georgia) Artillery
1st Richmond Howitzers
Troup (Georgia) Artillery

PICKETT'S DIVISION
Maj. Gen. George E. Pickett

Garnett's Brigade	*Kemper's Brigade*
Brig. Gen. R. B. Garnett	Brig. Gen. J. L. Kemper
Maj. C. S. Peyton	Col. Joseph Mayo, Jr.
8th Virginia	1st Virginia
18th Virginia	3rd Virginia
19th Virginia	7th Virginia
28th Virginia	11th Virginia
56th Virginia	24th Virginia

Armistead's Brigade
Brig. Gen. L. A. Armistead
Col. W. R. Aylett

9th Virginia
14th Virginia
38th Virginia
53rd Virginia
57th Virginia

Artillery
Maj. James Dearing

Fauquier (Virginia) Artillery
Hampden (Virginia) Artillery
Richmond Fayette Artillery
Virginia Battery

HOOD'S DIVISION
Maj. Gen. John B. Hood
Brig. Gen. E. M. Law

Law's Brigade	*Robertson's Brigade*
Brig. Gen. E. M. Law	Brig. Gen. J. B. Robertson
Col. James L. Sheffield	

4th Alabama	3rd Arkansas
15th Alabama	1st Texas
44th Alabama	4th Texas
47th Alabama	5th Texas
48th Alabama	

Anderson's Brigade	*Benning's Brigade*
Brig. Gen. George T. Anderson	Brig. Gen. Henry L. Benning
Lt. Col. William Luffman	

7th Georgia	2nd Georgia
8th Georgia	15th Georgia
9th Georgia	17th Georgia
11th Georgia	20th Georgia
59th Georgia	

Artillery

Maj. M. W. Henry

Branch (North Carolina) Artillery
German (South Carolina) Artillery
Palmetto (South Carolina) Light Artillery
Rowan (North Carolina) Artillery

ARTILLERY RESERVE
Col. J. B. Walton

Alexander's Battalion	*Washington (Louisiana) Artillery*
Col. E. P. Alexander	Maj. B. F. Eshleman

Ashland (Virginia) Artillery	First Company
Bedford (Virginia) Artillery	Second Company
Brooks (South Carolina) Artillery	Third Company
Madison (Louisiana) Light Artillery	Fourth Company
Virginia Battery	
Virginia Battery	

II CORPS
Lt. Gen. Richard S. Ewell

Escort
Randolph's Company Virginia Cavalry

EARLY'S DIVISION
Maj. Gen. Jubal A. Early

Hay's Brigade	*Smith's Brigade*
Brig. Gen. Harry T. Hays	Brig. Gen. William Smith

5th Louisiana
6th Louisiana
7th Louisiana
8th Louisiana
9th Louisiana

31st Virginia
49th Virginia
52nd Virginia

Hoke's Brigade
Col. Isaac E. Avery
Col. A. C. Godwin

6th North Carolina
21st North Carolina
57th North Carolina

Gordon's Brigade
Brig. Gen. J. B. Gordon

13th Georgia
26th Georgia
31st Georgia
38th Georgia
60th Georgia
61st Georgia

Artillery
Lt. Col. H. P. Jones

Charlottesville (Virginia) Artillery
Courtney (Virginia) Artillery
Louisiana Guard Artillery
Staunton (Virginia) Artillery

JOHNSON'S DIVISION
Maj. Gen. Edward Johnson

Steuart's Brigade
Brig. Gen. George H. Steuart

1st Maryland Battalion Infantry
1st North Carolina
3rd North Carolina
10th Virginia
23rd Virginia
37th Virginia

Nicholls' Brigade
Col. J. M. Williams

1st Louisiana
2nd Louisiana
10th Louisiana
14th Louisiana
15th Louisiana

Stonewall's Brigade
Brig. Gen. James A. Walker

2nd Virginia
4th Virginia
5th Virginia
27th Virginia
33rd Virginia

Jones' Brigade
Brig. Gen. John M. Jones'
Lt. Col. R. H. Dungan

21st Virginia
25th Virginia
42nd Virginia
44th Virginia
48th Virginia
50th Virginia

Artillery
Maj. J. W. Latimer
Capt. C. I. Raine

1st Maryland Battery
Alleghany (Virginia) Artillery
Chesapeake (Maryland) Artillery
Lee (Virginia) Battery

RODES' DIVISION
Maj. Gen. R. E. Rodes

Daniel's Brigade
Brig. Gen. Junius Daniel

32nd North Carolina
43rd North Carolina
45th North Carolina
53rd North Carolina
2nd North Carolina Battalion

Iverson's Brigade
Brig. Gen. Alfred Iverson

5th North Carolina
12th North Carolina
20th North Carolina
23rd North Carolina

Doles' Brigade
Brig. Gen. George Doles

4th Georgia
12th Georgia
21st Georgia
44th Georgia

Ramseur's Brigade
Brig. Gen. S. D. Ramseur

2nd North Carolina
4th North Carolina
14th North Carolina
30th North Carolina

O'Neal's Brigade
Col. E. A. O'Neal

3rd Alabama
5th Alabama
6th Alabama
12th Alabama
26th Alabama

Artillery
Lt. Col. Thomas H. Carter

Jeff Davis (Alabama) Artillery
King William (Virginia) Artillery
Morris (Virginia) Artillery
Orange (Virginia) Artillery

ARTILLERY RESERVE
Col. J. Thompson Brown

1st Virginia Artillery
Capt. Willis J. Dance

2nd Richmond (Virginia) Howitzers
3rd Richmond (Virginia) Howitzers
Powhatan (Virginia) Artillery
Rockbridge (Virginia) Artillery
Salem (Virginia) Artillery

Nelson's Battalion
Lt. Col. William Nelson

Amherst (Virginia) Artillery
Fluvanna (Virginia) Artillery
Georgia Battery

III CORPS
Lt. Gen. Ambrose P. Hill

ANDERSON'S DIVISION
Maj. Gen. R. H. Anderson

Wilcox's Brigade
Brig. Gen. Cadmus M. Wilcox

8th Alabama
9th Alabama
10th Alabama
11th Alabama
14th Alabama

Wright's Brigade
Brig. Gen. A. R. Wright
Col. Wllliam Gibson
Brig. Gen. A. R. Wright

3rd Georgia
22nd Georgia
48th Georgia
2nd Georgia Battalion

Mahone's Brigade
Brig. Gen. William Mahone

6th Virginia
12th Virginia
16th Virginia
41st Virginia
61st Virginia

Perry's Brigade
Col. David Lang

2nd Florida
5th Florida
8th Florida

Posey's Brigade
Brig. Gen. Carnot Posey

12th Mississippi
16th Mississippi
19th Mississippi
48th Mississippi

Artillery (Sumter Battalion)
Maj. John Lane

Company A
Company B
Company C

HETH'S DIVISION
Maj. Gen. Henry Heth
Brig. Gen. J. J. Pettigrew

1st Brigade	*3rd Brigade*
Brig. Gen. J. J. Pettigrew	Brig. Gen. James J. Archer
Col. J. K. Marshall	Col. B. D. Fry
	Lt. Col. S. G. Shepard
11th North Carolina	13th Alabama
26th North Carolina	5th Alabama Battalion
47th North Carolina	1st Tennessee (Provisional Army)
52nd North Carolina	7th Tennessee
	14th Tennessee
2nd Brigade	*4th Brigade*
Col. J. M. Brockenbrough	Brig. Gen. Joseph R. Davis
40th Virginia	2nd Mississippi
47th Virginia	11th Mississippi
55th Virginia	42nd Mississippi
22nd Virginia Battalion	55th North Carolina

Artillery
Lt. Col. John J. Garnett

Donaldsonville (Louisiana) Artillery
Huger (Virginia) Artillery
Lewis (Virginia) Artillery
Norfolk Light Artillery Blues

PENDER'S DIVISION
Maj. Gen. William D. Pender
Brig. Gen. James H. Lane
Maj. Gen. I. R. Trimble
Brig. Gen. James H. Lane

1st Brigade	*3rd Brigade*
Col. Abner Perrin	Brig. Gen. Edwad L. Thomas

1st South Carolina (Provisional Army)
1st South Carolina Rifles
12th South Carolina
13th South Carolina
14th South Carolina

14th Georgia
35th Georgia
45th Georgia
49th Georgia

2nd Briagde

Brig. Gen. James H. Lane
Col. C. M. Avery
Brig. Gen. James H. Lane
Col. C. M. Avery

4th Brigade

Brig. Gen. A. M. Scales
Lt. Col. G. T. Gordon
Col. W. Lee J. Lowrance

7th North Carolina
18th North Carolina
28th North Carolina
33rd North Carolina
37th North Carolina

13th North Carolina
16th North Carolina
22nd North Carolina
34th North Carolina
38th North Carolina

Artillery

Maj. William T. Poague

Albemarle (Virginia) Artillery
Charlotte (North Carolina) Artillery
Madison (Mississippi) Light Artillery
Virginia Battery

ARTILLERY RESERVE

Col. R. Lindsay Walker

McIntosh's Battalion

Maj. D. G. McIntosh

Pegram's Battalion

Maj. W. J. Pegram
Capt. E. B. Brunson

Danville (Virginia) Artillery
Hardaway (Alabama) Artillery
2nd Rockbridge (Virginia) Artillery
Virginia Battery

Crenshaw (Virginia) Battery
Fredericksburg (Virginia) Artillery
Letcher (Virginia) Artillery
Pee Dee (South Carolina) Artillery
Purcell (Virginia) Artillery

CAVALRY
STUART'S DIVISION
Maj. Gen. J. E. B. Stuart

Hampton's Brigade

Brig. Gen.Wade Hampton
Col. L. S. Baker

Fitz Lee's Brigade

Brig. Gen. Fitz. Lee

1st North Carolina
1st South Carolina
2nd South Carolina
Cobb's (Georgia) Legion
Jeff Davis Legion
Phillips (Georgia) Legion

1st Maryland Battalion
1st Virginia
2nd Virginia
3rd Virginia
4th Virginia
5th Virginia

Robertson's Brigade
Brig. Gen. Beverly H. Robertson

Jenkins' Brigade
Brig. Gen. A. G. Jenkins
Col. M. J. Ferguson

4th North Carolina
5th North Carolina

14th Virginia
16th Virginia
17th Virginia
34th Virginia Battalion
36th Virginia Battalion
Jackson's (Virginia) Battery

Jones' Brigade
Brig. Gen. William E. Jones

W. H. F. Lee's Brigade
Col. J. R. Chambliss, Jr

6th Virginia
7th Virginia
11th Virginia

2nd North Carolina
9th Virginia
10th Virginia
13th Virginia

Stuart's Horse Artillery
Maj. R. F. Beckham

Breathed's (Virginia) Battery
Chew's (Virginia) Battery
Griffin's (Maryland) Battery
Hart's (South Carolina) Battery
McGregor's (Virginia) Battery
Moorman's (Virginia) Battery

IMBODEN'S COMMAND
Brig. Gen. J. D. Imboden

18th Virginia Cavalry
62nd Virginia Infantry, Mounted
Virginia Partisan Rangers
Virginia Battery

Endnotes

WAYS AND MEANS

1. E. B. Long and Barbara Long, *The Civil War Day by Day: An Almanac 1861-1865.* (New York: Doubleday and Company, Inc., 1971), p. 705.
2. Ibid., p. 711. Includes all causes.
3. Frank A. Haskell, *The Battle of Gettysburg.* (Boston: Houghton Mifflin Company, 1958), p. 156.
4. William Roscoe Livermore, *The Story of the Civil War: A Concise Account of the War in the United States of America between 1861 and 1865, in the Continuation of the Story by John Codman Ropes.* Part III: The Campaigns of 1863 to July 10. Book II: Vicksburg, Port Hudson, Tullahoma, and Gettysburg. (New York: G.P. Putnam's Sons, 1913), p. 414.
5. Ibid., p. 413.
6. Russell F. Weigley, *The American Way Of War: A History of United Sates Military Strategy and Policy.* (New York: Macmillan Publishing Co., Inc., 1973), p. 106.
7. M. Jay Luvaas and Col. Harold W. Nelson. *The U.S. Army War College Guide to the Battle of Gettysburg.* (Carlisle, Pa: South Mountain Press, Inc., 1986), p. 204. See also Richard A. Preston and Sydney F. Wise. *Men in Arms* (New York: Holt, Rinehart and Winston, Inc., 1956 [1979]), p. 238, 247-48.
8. Major-General J. F. C. Fuller, *The Generalship of Alexander the Great.* (London: Eyre and Spottiswoode, 1958), p. 292. Fuller is actually explaining Alexander's battle tactics; however, the same tactics apply at Gettysburg.
9. Grady McWhiney and Perry D. Jamieson, *Attack and Die: Civil War Military Tactics and the Southern Heritage.* (University, Ala.: The University of Alabama Press, 1982), p. 49. See also, Cadmus M. Wilcox, *Rifles and Rifle Practice.* (New York: D. Van Nostrand, 1859), p. 243.
10. Harold L. Peterson. *Round Shot and Rammers.* (Bonanza Books, 1969), p. 119.
11. James Longstreet, "Lee's Invasion of Pennsylvania," *Battles and Leaders of the Civil War.* Eds. Robert U. Johnson and Clarence C. Buel. (New York: Castle, 1888), Vol. III, pp. 245-247. Cited hereafter as *B&L.*
12. Edwin B. Coddington, *The Gettysburg Campaign: A Study in Command.* (New York: Charles Scribner's Sons, 1968), p. 8.
13. *B&L*, Vol. III, p. 243.
14. George Gordon Meade, *The Battle of Gettysburg.* (York, Pa.: First Capitol Antiquarian Book and Paper Market, 1988), p. 11.
15. Information in this section is taken from: Meade, *The Battle*, p. 7; Coddington, *Gettysburg Campaign*, pp. 558-559; *B&L*, Vol. III, p. 256.

16. Gerald F. Linderman, *Embattled Courage: The Experience of Combat in the American Civil War.* (New York: The Free Press, 1989), p. 73.
17. Ibid.
18. All information in this section is taken from: *The War of the Rebellion: A Compilation of the Official Records of the Union and Confederate Armies.* Ser. I, Vol. XXVII, pt. 2. (Washington, D.C., Government Printing Office, 1880-1901), pp. 692-697 (cited hereafter as OR); *B&L*. Vol. III, pp. 251-253; Meade, *The Battle*, p. 9; Elisha Hunt Rhodes, *All for the Union.* Robert Hunt Rhodes, ed. (New York: Orion Books, 1991); Albert A. Nofi, *The Gettysburg Campaign: June and July, 1863.* (New York: W. H. Smith Publishers Inc., 1986), pp. 44-45.
19. Coddington, *Gettysburg Campaign*, p. 109-10.
20. Ibid., pp. 108-109.

TOUR I: STOP 1

21. OR, XXVII, pt. 2, p. 637.
22. Coddington, *Gettysburg Campaign*, p. 683.
23. OR, XXVII, pt. 1, p. 924.
24. Ibid., p. 114.
25. Albert Hard, M.D., *History of the 8th Cavalry Regiment Illinois Volunteers: During the Great Rebellion.* (Aura: Illinois Press, 1868), p. 257.
26. Bruce Catton, *Glory Road.* (Garden City, N.Y.: Doubleday and Company, Inc., 1952), p. 273. See also Catton's footnote 7, p. 372.
27. There seems to be a major discrepancy concerning the numbers of prisoners. General Doubleday (U.S.A.) states in his official report that 1000 Confederates were captured; OR, XXVII, pt. 1, p. 245. Confederate General Heth, on the other hand, says only 60 or 70 were taken captive; OR, XXVII, pt. 2, p. 638.

TOUR I: STOP 3

28. Ibid.
29. Coddington, *Gettysburg Campaign*, p. 271.
30. Ibid., p. 272.
31. Catton, *Glory Road*, p. 274.
32. OR, XXVII, pt. 1, p. 276.

TOUR I: STOP 4

33. Ibid., p. 249.

TOUR I: STOP 5

34. Ibid., pt. 2, p. 579.
35. Walter Clark, ed., *Histories of the Several Regiments and Battalions from North Carolina in the Great War 1861-65*. Vol. 2. (Raleigh, N.C.: Broadfoot's Bookmark, 1982), pp. 235-237.

TOUR I: STOP 6

36. Catherine Merrill, *Indiana Soldier in the War for the Union*. (Indianapolis: Merrill and Company, 1869), pp. 106-107.
37. OR, XXVII, pt. 1, p. 927.
38. Ibid.
39. Ibid., p. 445.
40. Champ Clark, *Gettysburg: The Confederate High Tide*. (Alexandria, Va.: Time-Life Books, 1985), p. 67.
41. Ibid, p. 62.
42. OR, XXVII, pt. 1, p. 173. See also O. B. Curtis. *History of the Twenty-Fourth Michigan of the Iron Brigade, known as the Detroit and Wayne County Regiment*. (Detroit: Winn and Hammond, 1891), p. 167. His calculations are somewhat exaggerated when compared to the Official Reports.
43. John W. Busey and David G. Martin, *Regimental Strengths and Losses at Gettysburg*. (Hightstown, N.J.: Longstreet House, 1982), pp. 239-292. See also John M. Vanderslice. *Gettysburg: Then and Now. The Field of American Valor Where and How the Regiments Fought and the Troops they Encountered*. (New York: G. W. Dillingham Co., 1899), pp. 120 and 132.
44. All information in this section is taken from OR, XXVII, pt. 2, pp. 318-319.
45. Coddington, *Gettysburg Campaign*, pp. 337-338.
46. Nofi, *Gettysburg Campaign*, p. 74.

TOUR II: STOP 7

47. George Stewart, *Pickett's Charge: A Microhistory of the Final Attack at Gettysburg, July 3, 1863*. (Dayton, Ohio: Morningside Bookshop, 1983), pp. ix and 263.

TOUR II: STOP 8

48. Ibid., p. 257.

TOUR II: STOP 9

49. B&L, p. 319.
50. Harry W. Pfanz, *Gettysburg: The Second Day*. (Chapel Hill, N.C.: The University of North Carolina Press, 1987), p. 178.
51. Captain Calvin L. Collier, *"They'll Do To Tie To!" The Story of the Third Regiment, Arkansas Infantry, Confederate States of America*. (Little Rock, AK: Eagle Press, 1959), p. 138.
52. Ibid., pp. 138-139.

TOUR II: STOP 10A

53. John J. Pullen, *The Twentieth Maine: A Volunteer Regiment in the Civil War*. (Dayton, Ohio: Morningside Bookshop, 1983), p. 111.
54. Ibid., p. 119.
55. William Calvin Oates, *The War Between the Union and the Confederacy and Its Lost Opportunities*. (New York: Morningside, 1974), p. 219.
56. Pullen, *Twentieth Maine*, pp. 119-120.

57. Ibid., p. 227.
58. OR, XXVII, pt. 1, p. 624.
59. Ibid.

TOUR II: STOP 10B

60. John C. West, *A Texan in Search of a Fight*. (Waco, Tx.: J. S. Hill and Company, 1901), p. 86.
61. Pfanz, *Second Day*, pp. 228-230.
62. Ibid., p. 230.
63. John W. Urban, Company D, First Regiment Pennsylvania Reserve Infantry. *In Defense of the Union; or, Through Shot and Shell and Prison Pen*. (Chicago/Philadelphia: Monarch Book Company, 1887), p. 317.
64. Pfanz, *Second Day*, p. 398.

TOUR II: STOP 11A

65. General W. F. Perry, "The Devil's Den," *Confederate Veteran*, (Nashville, Tenn.) Vol. 9, No. 4, April 1901, p. 161.
66. Kathleen Georg Harrison, "Our Principal Loss was in this Place, Action at the Slaughter Pen and at South end of Houck's Ridge, Gettysburg, Pennsylvania, 2 July, 1863," *Gettysburg Magazine*, July 1989, p. 62.
67. Captain James E. Smith, *A Famous Battery and Its Campaigns, 1861-64*. (Washington, D.C.: W. H. Lowdermilk and Co., 1892), p. 140.
68. Pfanz, *Second Day*, p. 199.

TOUR II: STOP 11B

69. Ibid, p. 103.
70. Charles H. Weygant, *History of the One Hundred and Twenty-Fourth Regiment, N.Y.S.V.* (Gaithersburg, Md.: Journal Printing House, 1877), p. 176.
71. Ibid, p. 177. See also Harrison, p. 59.
72. Pfanz, *Second Day*, p. 195.

TOUR II: STOP 12

73. Ibid., pp. 250-251.
74. Philippe Regis Denis de Keredern, comte Trobriand, *Four Years with the Army of the Potomac*. trans. George K. Dauchy. (Boston: Ticknor and Company, 1889), p. 497.
75. Pfanz, *Second Day*, p. 273. See also William A. Child, *A History of the Fifth Regiment, New Hampshire Volunteers in the American Civil War*. (Bristol, N.H.: R.W. Musgrove, 1893), pp. 208-212.
76. Ibid.
77. St. Clair Augustin Mulholland, *The Story of the 116th Regiment Pennsylvania Volunteers in the War of the Rebellion*. (Philadelphia: F. McManus Jr. and Company, 1903), p. 125.
78. John P. Nicholson, ed. *Pennsylvania at Gettysburg: Ceremonies at the Dedication of the Monuments Erected by the Commonwealth of Pennsylvania*. 3 vols. (Harrisburg: Wm. Stanley Ray, 1904), Vol. 2, p. 629.
79. Mulholland, *116th Regiment*, pp. 126-127.
80. Winthrop D. Sheldon, A.M., *The "Twenty-Seventh." A Regimental History*. (New Haven: Morris and Benham, 1866), p. 91. See also John Niven, *Connecticut for the Union: The Role of the State in the Civil War*. (New Haven: Yale University Press, 1965), pp. 236-237.

81. Pfanz, *Second Day*, p. 293.
82. Ibid., p. 294. See also Pfanz's endnote 109 pp. 525-526.

TOUR II: STOP 13

83. Michael Hanifen, *History of Battery B, First New Jersey Artillery*. (Highstown, N.J.: Longstreet House, 1991), pp. 74-75.
84. D. Augustus Dickert, *History of Kershaw's Brigade with Complete Roll of Companies*. (Dayton, Ohio: Morningside Bookshop, 1973), p. 239.
85. Martin A. Haynes, *History of the Second Regiment New Hampshire Volunteers: Its Camps, Marches and Battles*. (Manchester, N.H.: Charles F. Livingston, 1865), pp. 141-144.
86. Richard Barnitz. "Return to Gettysburg." *American Legion Magazine*. 33 (July, 1942): pp. 24-25 & 38-41. Found in Robert Brake's Collection, Archives, U.S. Military History Institute, Carlisle, Pa.

TOUR II: STOP 14

87. Samuel Toombs, *New Jersey Troops in the Gettysburg Campaign: From June 5 To July 31, 1863*. (New Jersey: Longstreet House, 1988), pp. 237-240. See also, Pfanz, *Second Day*, pp. 368-371.
88. Vanderslice, *Then and Now*, pp. 111-112.

TOUR II: STOP 15

89. Major John Bigelow, *The Peach Orchard: Gettysburg July 2, 1863*. (Minneapolis: Kimball-Storer Co., 1910), pp. 56-60. See also Pfanz, *Second Day*, pp. 343-346.

TOUR II: STOP 16

90. Reverend William Corby, *Memoirs of Chaplain Life: Three Years Chaplain in the Famous Irish Brigade, "Army of the Potomac."* (Notre Dame, Scholastic Press, 1894), p. 183. Translation by Jennifer S. Andrews, Latin and History major, class of 1992, Dickinson College, Carlisle, Pa.

TOUR II STOP 17

91. Nofi, *Gettysburg Campaign*, p. 119.
92. Coddington, *Gettysburg Campaign*, p. 423.
93. Account of the 1st Minnesota attack is cited from the Robert L. Brake Collection, Archives, U.S. Army Military History Institute.
94. OR, XXVII, pt. 1, 371.
95. Ibid., pt. 2, p. 619.

TOUR II: STOP 18

96. This conversation recorded in, E. R. Brown, *Twenty-Seventh Indiana Volunteer Infantry in the War of the Rebellion 1861 to 1865 First Division 12th and 20th Corps*. (Gaithersburg, Md.: Butternut Press, 1984), pp. 379-380.
97. Ibid, pp. 382-383.
98. Coddington, *Gettysburg Campaign*, p. 475.

TOUR II: STOP 19

99. W. W. Goldsborough, *The Maryland Line in the Confederate Army, 1861-1865*. (Gaithersburg, Md.: Butternut Press, 1900), pp. 103-104.
100. OR, XXVII, pt.1, pp. 856-857.
101. *Report of the State of Maryland, Gettysburg Monument Commission*. (Baltimore: William K. Boyle and Son, 1891), p. 58.
102. Goldsborough, *The Maryland Line*, p. 109.
103. Ibid, p. 110.
104. Vanderslice, *Then and Now*, p. 146.
105. Edward J. Stackpole, *They Met at Gettysburg*. (Harrisburg: The Stackpole Company, 1956), p. 243.

TOUR II: STOP 20

106. General James Longstreet, *From Manassas to Appomattox: Memoirs of the Civil War in America*. (New York: Mallard Press, 1991), p. 375.
107. Colonel Harry Gilmor, *Four Years in the Saddle*. (New York: Harper and Brothers, 1866), p. 99.
108. *Pennsylvania at Gettysburg*, Vol. II, p. 932.
109. Terry Jones, *Lee's Tigers: The Louisiana Infantry in the Army of Northern Virginia*. (Baton Rouge: Louisiana State University Press, 1987), pp. 170-174.

TOUR III: STOP 22

110. Meade, *Battle of Gettysburg*, p. 89.
111. Stewart, *Pickett's Charge*, p. 115.
112. Coddington, *Gettysburg Campaign*, p. 494.
113. Ibid.
114. Stewart, *Pickett's Charge*, p. 139.
115. David E. Johnston, *Four Years a Soldier*. (Princeton: W.V., 1887), p. 253.
116. Coddington, *Gettysburg Campaign*, p. 498.
117. Ibid. p. 500.
118. Stewart, *Pickett's Charge*, p. 173.
119. Ibid., p. 174.

TOUR III: STOP 23A

120. Ibid.
121. Haskell, *Battle of Gettysburg*, p. 96.
122. Taken from Robert Brake's collection from Randolph A. Shotwell, 8th Regiment Virginia Volunteers. Virginia and North Carolina in the Battle of Gettysburg. "Southern Historical Monthly." pp. 112-113.
123. Stewart, *Pickett's Charge*, p. 187.
124. Ralph Orson Sturtevant, *Pictorial History of the Thirteenth Regiment Vermont Volunteers, War of 1861-1865*. (Burlington, Vt.: The Free Press, 1910), pp. 305-307.
125. Ibid.
126. Johnston, *Four Years*, p. 259.
127. Coddington, *Gettysburg Campaign*, pp. 527-28.

TOUR III: STOP 23B

128. Ibid., p. 516.
129. Clark, *Gettysburg*, p. 141.

TOUR III: STOP 23C

130. D. Scott Hartwig. "It Struck Horror To Us All," *The Gettysburg Magazine*, January 1991, no. 4, p. 98.
131. Clark, *Gettysburg*, p. 141.
132. Lieutenant J. Irving Sale, *The Philadelphia Press*, 4 July 1887, p. 1, column 1. Citation found in Robert Brake's Collection, the New York 1st Independent Battery, Artillery, folder, in Archives, Military History Institute, Carlisle, Pa.
133. Haskell, *Battle of Gettysburg*, p. 104; see also Coddington, *Gettysburg Campaign*, p. 518.
134. *History of the Nineteenth Regiment: Massachusetts Volunteer Infantry, 1861-1865*. (Salem: Salem Press Co., 1906), p. 242.
135. Wayne E. Motts, "*Trust In God And Fear Nothing*," *General Lewis A Armistead, CSA*. (Farnsworth House Military Impression, 1994), p. 49. See also, T. C. Holland, "With Armistead at Gettysburg," CV, Vol. 29, 1921 p. 62.

TOUR III: STOP 23D

136. Thomas M. Aldrich, *The History of Battery A, First Rhode Island Light Artillery in the War to Preserve the Union 1861-1865*. (Providence: Snow and Farnham, 1904), p. 216.

TOUR III: STOP 23E

137. Clark, *Gettysburg*, Vol. II., pp. 356-58.
138. Toombs, *New Jersey Troops*, p. 300.
139. Maud Morrow Brown, *The University Greys, Company A Eleventh Mississippi Regiment Army of Northern Virginia 1862-1865*. (Richmond, Va.: Garrett and Massie, 1940), p. 46.

140. Franklin Sawyer. *A Military History of the 8th Regiment Ohio Volunteer Infantry: Its Battles, Marches and Army Movements.* George A. Groot, ed. (Cleveland: Fairbanks and Co., 1881), pp. 131-132.
141. For another location of Pickett and his staff during the charge see, Kathleen R. Georg and John W. Busey. *Nothing But Glory: Pickett's Division at Gettysburg*. (Hightstown, N.J.: Longstreet House, 1987), p. 202.
142. This conversation can be found in Stewart, *Pickett's Charge*, pp. 256-257.
143. Ibid.
144. Ibid.
145. Ibid., p. 266.
146. See note 105 in Gregory A. Coco, ed., *On The Bloodstained Field: 130 Human Interest Stories of the Campaign and Battle of Gettysburg*. (Gettysburg: Thomas Publications, 1987), p. 55.
147. Coddington, *Gettysburg Campaign*, p. 522

TOUR III: SUMMARY

148. Mark Boatner III, *The Civil War Dictionary*. (New York: Vintage Books, 1991), p. 339. See also Thomas Livermore, *Numbers and Losses in the Civil War in America 1861-1865*.(Boston, 1900).

CONCLUSION: STOP 24

149. Nofi, *Gettysburg Campaign*, p. 187.

APPENDIX A

150. Long, E. B., pp. 711-12.

Photographs Bibliography

Unless otherwise noted, photographs are courtesy of the United States Military History Institute, Carlisle Barracks, Carlisle, Pennsylvania, Photo Archivists Michael J. Winey and Randy Hackenburg.

Additional photographs reproduced from:

Lt. Marcellus Jones:	Hard, Albert, M.D. *History of the 8th Cavalry Regiment Illinois Volunteers: During the Great Rebellion.* Aura: Illinois Press, 1868, p. XXV.
Blacknall: Johnson: Christie: Wagg:	Clark, Walter, ed. *Histories of the Several Regiments and Battalions from North Carolina in the Great War 1861-65.* Vol. 2 Goldsboro, N.C.: Nash Brothers, Book and Job Printers, 1901 (opposite p. 181).
Pvt. John C. West:	West, John C. *A Texan in Search of a Fight.* Waco, Tx.: J. S. Hill and Company, 1901. Photo before introduction.
Col. William F. Perry:	*Confederate Veteran*
Brig. Gen. George Benning: Brig. Gen. W. T. Wofford:	Miller, Francis T., ed. *Photographic History of the Civil War.* 10 vols. New York: 1911. Vol. 10.
Lt. Col. Merwin:	Sheldon, Winthrop D., A.M. *The "Twenty-Seventh:" A Regimental History.* New Haven: Morris and Benham, 1866, inside cover.
Capt. Clark: Clairville: Timm: Michael Hanifen:	Hanifen, Michael. *History of Battery B: First New Jersey Artillery.* Ottawa, Il.: Republican-Times, Printers, 1905, Clark. inside cover, p. 72.
Capt. Theodore Malloy:	Dickert, D. Augustus. *History of Kershaw's Brigade with Complete Roll of Companies.* Newberry, S.C.: Elbert H. Aull Company, 1899, opposite p. 345.
Lt. Dascomb: Hubbard:	Haynes, Prvt. Martin A. *History of the Second Regiment, New Hampshire Volunteers: Its Camps, Marches and Battles.* Manchester, N.H.: Charles F. Livingston, 1865, Dascomb, p. 170; Hubbard, p. 182.
Kearney:	Marbaker, Sergeant Thomas D., Company E. *History of the Eleventh New Jersey Volunteers: From Its Organization to Appomattox.* Trenton, N.J.: Maccrellish & Quigley, 1898, p. 26.
Murray:	Howard, McHenry. *Recollections of a Confederate Staff Officer.* Williams and Wilkens Co., 1914, p. 3a.
Thomas F. McKie:	Brown, Maud Morrow. *The University Greys: Company A Eleventh Mississippi Regiment Army of Northern Virginia, 1861-1865.* Richmond: Garrett and Massie, Inc., 1940, inside cover.
Private Wesley Culp:	Gettysburg National Park
Col. David Lang:	Valentine Museum

Bibliography

Aldrich, Thomas M. *The History of Battery A, First Rhode Island Light Artillery in the War to Preserve the Union 1861-1865.* Providence: Snow and Farnham, 1904.

Alexander, Edward P. *Fighting for the Confederacy: The Personal Recollections of General Edward Porter Alexander.* Gary W. Gallagher, ed. Chapel Hill: The University of North Carolina Press, 1989.

Arnold-Friend, Louise. *Gettysburg Campaign and Battle, June-July, 1863: A Working Bibliography.* Carlisle: U.S. Army Military History Institute, 1993.

Banes, Charles H. *History of the Philadelphia Brigade.* Philadelphia: J. B. Lippincott & Co., 1876. U.S. Army Military History Institute, Carlisle, Pa.

Barnitz, Richard. "Return to Gettysburg." *American Legion Magazine.* 33 (July 1942): pp. 24-25 and 38-41.

Barton, Michael. *Goodmen: The Character of the Civil War Soldiers.* University College, Pa: Pennsylvania State University Press, 1981.

Bigelow, Major John (Captain, 9th Mass. Battery). *The Peach Orchard, Gettysburg, July 2, 1863: Explained by Official Reports and Maps.* Minneapolis: Kimball-Storer Co., 1910. U.S. Military History Institute, Carlisle, Pa.

Boyd, Charles. *The Devil's Den: A History of the 44th Alabama Volunteer Infantry Regiment Confederate States Army, 1862-1865.* Birmingham, Ala.: Banner Press, 1987.

Brake, Robert L. Collection, Archives, U.S. Army Military History Institute; St. Clair Mulholland, *The Story of the 116th Pennsylvania*; Walter F. Beyer and O. F. Keydel, *Deeds of Valor*; Ida Lee Johnston "Over the Stone Wall at Gettysburg," *Confederate Veteran*, vol. XXXI, p. 249; Wm. R. Kiefer, *History of the 153rd Pennsylvania*.

Brown, E. R. *The Twenty-Seventh Indiana Volunteer Infantry in the War of the Rebellion: 1861 to 1865, First Division 12th and 20th Corps.* Gaithersburg, Md.: Butternut Press, 1899. U.S. Army Military History Institute, Carlisle, Pa.

Brown, Maud Morrow. *The University Greys: Company A Eleventh Mississippi Regiment Army of Northern Virginia, 1861-1865.* Richmond: Garrett and Massie, Inc., 1940.

Bruce, George A. Brevet-Lieutenant Colonel. *The Twentieth Regiment of Massachusetts Volunteer Infantry 1861-1865.* New York: Houghton, Mifflin and Company, 1906.

Busey, John W. and David G. Martin. *Regimental Strengths at Gettysburg.* Baltimore: Gateway Press, 1982.

Campbell, Eric. "Caldwell Clears the Wheatfield." *Gettysburg Magazine.* 3 (July 1990): pp. 27-50.

_____. "`Remember Harper's Ferry': The Degradation, Humiliation, and Redemption of Col. George L. Willard's Brigade, Part 2." *Gettysburg Magazine.* 8 (Jan. 1993): pp. 95-111.

Carpenter, Alfred P., Co. K, First Minnesota Volunteers Infantry. "Letter on the Battle of Gettysburg, Warrenton Junction, Va., 30 July, 1863. Minnesota Historical Society: From Robert Brake Collection, U.S. Army Military History Institute, Carlisle, Pa.

Catton, Bruce. *Glory Road.* Garden City, N.Y.: Doubleday and Company, Inc., 1952.

Child, William A. *A History of the Fifth Regiment, New Hampshire Volunteers in the American Civil War.* Bristol, N.H.: R.W. Musgrove, 1893.

Clark, Champ. *Gettysburg: The Confederate High Tide.* Alexandria, Va.: Time Life Book Series, 1985.

Clark, Walter, ed. *Histories of the Several Regiments and Battalions from North Carolina in the Great War 1861-65.* Vol. 2. Goldsboro, N.C.: Nash Brothers, Book and Job Printers, 1901.

Coco, Gregory A., ed. *On the Bloodstained Field: 130 Human Interest Stories of the Campaign and Battle of Gettysburg.* Gettysburg: Thomas Publications, 1987.

_____, ed. *On the Bloodstained Field II: 132 More Human Interest Stories of the Campaign and Battle of Gettysburg.* Gettysburg: Thomas Publications, 1989.

Coddington, Edwin B. *The Gettysburg Campaign: A Study in Command.* New York: Charles Scribner's Sons, 1968.

Colvill, William Jr., Colonel First Minnesota. "Account of Colonel Colvill at the Battle of Gettysburg." Letter to the Editor, *The Minneapolis Daily Tribune* 28 July, 1884. From the Robert L. Brake Collection, U.S. Army Military History Institute, Carlisle, Pa.

Collier, Captain Calvin L. *"They'll Do To Tie To!" The Story of the Third Regiment, Arkansas Infantry, Confederate States of America.* Little Rock, Ark.: Eagle Press, 1959.

Corby, William, Rev. *Memoirs of Chaplain Life: Three Years Chaplain in the Famous Irish Brigade, "Army of the Potomac".* Notre Dame: Scholastic Press, 1894.

Cowan, Andrew, Capt. of the 1st New York Battery. Undated remarks by Andrew Cowan . . . in response to Alexander Stewart Webb . . . on a sketch of the repulse of Pickett's Charge. Alexander Stewart Webb Collection, Yale University Library. U.S. Army Military History Institute, Carlisle, Pa.

Curtis, O.B. *History of the Twenty-Fourth Michigan of the Iron Brigade, Known as the Detroit and Wayne County Regiment.* Detroit: Winn and Hammond, 1891.

de Trobriand, Regis. *Four Years with the Army of the Potomac.* trans. George K. Dauchy. Boston: Ticknor and Company, 1889.

Dickert, D. Augustus. *History of Kershaw's Brigade with Complete Roll of Companies.* Newberry, S.C.: Elbert H. Aull Company, 1899.

Divine, John E. (ed.) *8th Virginia Infantry.* Lynchburg, Va.: H.E. Howard, Inc., 1983. U.S. Army Military History Institute, Carlisle, Pa.

Dowdey, Clifford. *Death of a Nation: The Story of Lee and His Men at Gettysburg.* New York: Alfred A. Knopf, 1958.

Downey, Fairfax. *The Guns at Gettysburg.* New York: David McKay Company Inc., 1958.

Elmore, Thomas L. "Courage Against the Trenches: The Attack and Repulse of Steuart's Brigade on Culp's Hill." *Gettysburg Magazine.* 7 (July 1992): pp. 83-97.

Evans, Gen. Clement A. (ed.) *Confederate Military History Extended Edition.* 17 Vols. Wilmington, N.C.: Broadfoot Pub. Co., 1987 [1899]. U.S. Army Military History Institute, Carlisle, Pa.

Fuller, J.F.C. Major-General. *The Generalship of Alexander the Great.* London: Eyre and Spottiswoode, 1958.

Gaff, Alan D. "The Indiana Relief Effort at Gettysburg." *Gettysburg Magazine.* 3 (July 1990): pp. 109-115.

Georg, Kathleen R. and John W. Busey. *Nothing But Glory: Pickett's Division at Gettysburg.* David G. Martin, ed. Hightstown, N.J.: Longstreet House, 1987.

Gilmor, Colonel Harry. *Four Years in the Saddle.* New York: Harper and Brothers, 1866.

Goldsborough, W.W. *The Maryland Line in the Confederate Army: 1861-1865.* Baltimore, Md.: Guggenheimer, Weil & Co., 1900. [Gaithersburg, Md.: Butternut Press, 1983]. U.S. Army Military History Institute, Carlisle, Pa.

Hanifen, Michael. *History of Battery B: First New Jersey Artillery.* Ottawa, Ill.: Republican-Times, Printers, 1905.

Hard, Albert, M.D. *History of the 8th Cavalry Regiment Illinois Volunteers: During the Great Rebellion.* Aura: Illinois Press, 1868.

Harrison, Kathy Georg. *The Location of the Monuments, Markers, and Tablets on Gettysburg Battlefield.* Gettysburg: Thomas Publications, 1993.

_____. "`Our Principal Loss Was in This Place': Action at the Slaughter Pen and the South End of Houck's Ridge, 2 July, 1863." *Gettysburg Magazine.* 1 (July 1989), pp. 45-70.

Hartwig, D. Scott. "It Struck Horror To Us All." *Gettysburg Magazine.* 4 (Jan. 1991): pp. 89-101.

Haskell, Frank A. *The Battle of Gettysburg.* Boston: Houghton Mifflin Company, 1958.

Haynes, Priv. Martin A. *History of the Second Regiment, New Hampshire Volunteers: Its Camps, Marches and Battles.* Manchester, N.H.: Charles F. Livingston, 1865. U.S. Army Military History Institute, Carlisle, Pa.

Herdegen, Lance J. and William J. K. Beaudot. *In the Bloody Railroad Cut at Gettysburg.* Dayton, Ohio: Morningside House, Inc. [1990] 1991.

History of the Nineteenth Regiment, Massachusetts Volunteer Infantry, 1861-1865. Salem, Mass.: The Salem Press Co., 1906. U.S. Army Military History Institute, Carlisle, Pa.

Hogg, Ian V. *Weapons of the Civil War.* New York: Military Press, distributed by Crown Pub., 1987.

Holcombe, Return I. *History of the First Regiment Minnesota Volunteer Infantry: 1861-1864.* Minnesota: Easto and Masterman, 1916.

Hoke, Jacob. *The Great Invasion of 1863 or General Lee in Pennsylvania.* Ohio: W. J. Shuey Publisher, 1887.

Hyde, Corporal James S. *The Gettysburg Campaign of the 137th New York.* Charles L. English, ed. Norwich Civil War Round Table Collection, U.S. Army Military History Institute, Carlisle, Pa.

Jones, Terry. *Lee's Tigers: The Louisiana Infantry in the Army of Northern Virginia.* Baton Rouge: Louisiana State University Press, 1987.

Johnston, David E. *Four Years a Soldier.* Princeton, W.V.: 1887. U.S. Army Military History Institute, Carlisle, Pa.

Lash, Gary G. "The Philadelphia Brigade at Gettysburg." *Gettysburg Magazine.* 7 (July 1992): pp. 97-114.

Lewis, John H. *Recollections from 1860 to 1865.* Washington, D.C.: Peake & Company, 1895. U.S. Army Military History Institute, Carlisle, Pa.

Linderman, Gerald F. *Embattled Courage: The Experience of Combat in the American Civil War.* New York: The Free Press, 1989.

Livermore, William Roscoe. *The Story of the Civil War: A Concise Account of the War in the United States of America Between 1861 and 1865, in the Continuation of the Story by John Codman Ropes.* Part III: The Campaigns of 1863 to July 10. Book II: Vicksburg, Port Hudson, Tullahoma, and Gettysburg. New York: G.P. Putnam's Sons, [1894] 1913.

Long, E. B. and Barbara Long. *The Civil War Day by Day: An Almanac 1861-1865.* New York: Doubleday and Company, Inc., 1971.

Longstreet, James. "Lee's Invasion of Pennsylvania." In *Battles and Leaders of the Civil War.* Vol. III., edited by Robert U. Johnson and Clarence C. Buel. New York: Castle, 1888.

_____. *From Manassas to Appomattox: Memoirs of the Civil War in America.* New York: Mallard Press, 1991.

Luvaas, M. Jay and Col. Harold W. Nelson. *The U.S. Army War College Guide to the Battle of Gettysburg.* Carlisle, Pa.: South Mountain Press, Inc., 1986.

Maine at Gettysburg: Report of the Maine Commissioners. Portland: Lakeside, 1898.

Marbaker, Sergeant Thomas D., Company E. *History of the Eleventh New Jersey Volunteers: From Its Organization to Appomattox.* Trenton, N.J.: MacCrellish & Quigley, 1898.

McWhiney, Grady and Perry D. Jamieson. *Attack and Die: Civil War Military Tactics and the Southern Heritage.* University, Ala.: The University of Alabama Press, 1982.

Meade, George Gordon. *The Battle of Gettysburg.* York, Pa.: First Capitol Antiquarian Book and Paper Market, 1988.

Merrill, Catherine. *Indiana Soldier in the War for the Union.* Indianapolis: Merrill and Company, 1869.

Michigan at Gettysburg. Detroit: Winn and Hammond, 1889.

Montgomery, James Stuart. *The Shaping of a Battle: Gettysburg.* Philadelphia: Chilton Company, 1959.

Motts, Wayne E. "To Gain A Second Star: The Forgotten George S. Greene." *Gettysburg Magazine.* 3 (July 1990), pp. 63-75.

_____. "Trust In God And Fear Nothing," General Lewis Armistead, CSA.* Gettysburg: Farnsworth House Military Impressions, 1994.

Mulholland, St. Clair Augustin. *The Story of the 116th Regiment Pennsylvania Volunteers in the War of the Rebellion: The Record of a Gallant Command.* Philadelphia: F. McManus Jr. and Company Printers, 1899.

Newman, Harry Wright. *Maryland and the Confederacy: An objective narrative of Maryland's participation in the War Between the States 1861-1865, with annotations of important personalities and vital events of the war.* Annapolis: Harry Wright Newman, 1976. U.S. Army Military History Institute, Carlisle, Pa.

New York Monuments Commission for the Battlefields of Gettysburg and Chattanooga. *Final Report on the Battlefield of Gettysburg*. 3 vols. Albany, N.Y.: J. B. Lyon Company, Printers, 1900.

Nicholson, John P., ed. *Pennsylvania at Gettysburg: Ceremonies at the Dedication of the Monuments Erected by the Commonwealth of Pennsylvania*. 3 vols. Harrisburg: Wm. Stanley Ray, State Printer, 1904.

Niven, John. *Connecticut for the Union: The Role of the State in the Civil War*. New Haven: Yale University Press, 1965.

Nofi, Albert A. *The Gettysburg Campaign: June and July, 1863*. New York: W. H. Smith Publishers, Inc., 1986.

Oates, William Calvin. *The War Between the Union and the Confederacy and Its Lost Opportunities*. New York: Morningside, 1974.

Osborn, Maj. Thomas Ward. *The Eleventh Corps Artillery at Gettysburg. The Papers of Major Thomas Ward Osborn Chief of Artillery*. Herb S. Crumb, ed. Hamilton, N.Y.: Edmonston Publishing, Inc., 1991. U.S. Army Military History Institute, Carlisle, Pa.

Peterson, Harold L. *Round Shot and Rammers*. Bonanza Books, 1969.

Perry, William F. "The Devil's Den." *Confederate Veteran*. Vol. 9, No. 4, Nashville, Tenn.: April 1901.

Pfanz, Harry W. *Gettysburg: The Second Day*. Chapel Hill, N.C.: University of North Carolina Press, 1987.

Philadelphia Press. 3 July, 1887, pg. 2, col. 4. From Brake Collection, U.S. Army Military History Institute, Carlisle, Pa.

Philadelphia Press. 4 July, 1887, pg. 1, col. 6. From Brake Collection, U.S. Army Military History Institute, Carlisle, Pa.

Phipps, Michael and John S. Peterson. *"The Devil's To Pay" General John Buford, USA*. Gettysburg: Farnsworth Military Impressions, 1995.

Plummer, John W. Sergeant Co. D, First Minnesota Volunteer Infantry, "Letter to His Brother," *State Atlas*, Minneapolis, 26 August 1863: From the Brake Collection, U.S. Army Military History Institute, Carlisle, Pa.

Preston, Richard A. and Sydney F. Wise. *Men in Arms: A History of Warfare and Its Interrelationships with Western Society*. N.Y.: Holt, Rinehart and Winston, Inc., [1956] 1979.

Pullen, John J. *The Twentieth Maine: A Volunteer Regiment in the Civil War*. Dayton, Ohio: Morningside Bookshop, 1983.

Quint, Alonzo H. *The Record of the Second Massachusetts Infantry, 1861-65*. Boston: James P. Walker, 1867.

"Report of the State of Maryland: Gettysburg Monument Commission." Baltimore: William K. Boyle & Son, 1891. U.S. Army Military History Institute, Carlisle, Pa.

Rhodes, Elisha Hunt. *All For the Union: The Civil War Diary and Letters of Elisha Hunt Rhodes*, Robert Hunt Rhodes, ed. New York: Orion Books, 1991 [1985].

Saint Paul's Daily Press, 25 July, 1863, pg. 1. From Brake Collection, U.S. Army Military History Institute, Carlisle, Pa.

Sale, Lt. J. Irving. *The Philadelphia Press*, 4 July, 1887, p. 1, column 1. Citation found in Robert Brake's Collection, the New York 1st Independent Battery, Artillery, in Archives, U.S. Military History Institute, Carlisle, Pa.

Sawyer, Franklin. *A Military History of the 8th Regiment Ohio Volunteer Infantry: Its Battles, Marches and Army Movements*. George A. Groot, ed. Cleveland: Fairbanks & Co., 1881. U.S. Military History Institute, Carlisle, Pa.

Sheldon, Winthrop D., A.M. *The "Twenty-Seventh:" A Regimental History*. New Haven: Morris and Benham, 1866.

Smith, James. *A Famous Battery and its Campaigns, 1861-'64*. Washington, D.C.: W. H. Lowdermilk and Co., 1892.

Stackpole, Edward J. *They Met at Gettysburg*. Harrisburg, Pa.: The Stackpole Company, 1956.

Stanchak, John E. Ed. "Gettysburg: The Full Story of the Struggle," *The Civil War Times*. Harrisburg, Pa.: Historical Times Inc., 1988.

Stewart, George R. *Pickett's Charge: A Microhistory of the Final Attack at Gettysburg, July 3, 1863*. Dayton, Ohio: Morningside Bookshop, 1983.

Street, James, Jr. *The Struggle for Tennessee: Tupelo to Stones River*. Alexandria, Va.: Time Life Books, 1985.

Sturtevant, Ralph Orson. *Pictorial History Thirteenth Regiment Vermont Volunteers, War of 1861-1865*. Burlington, Vt.: The Free Press Association, 1910.

Taylor, Michael W. "North Carolina in the Pickett-Pettigrew-Trimble Charge at Gettysburg." *Gettysburg Magazine*. 8 (Jan. 1993): pp. 67-95.

Toombs, Samuel. *New Jersey Troops in the Gettysburg Campaign from June 5 to July 31, 1863*. Reprint No. 202. New Jersey: Longstreet House, 1988. U.S. Army Military History Institute, Carlisle, Pa.

Urban, John W., Co. D, First Regiment Pennsylvania Reserve Infantry. *In Defense of the Union; or, Through Shot and Shell and Prison Pen*. Chicago/Philadelphia: Monarch Book Company, 1887.

Vanderslice, John M. *Gettysburg: Then and Now: The Field of American Valor Where and How the Regiments Fought and the Troops They Encountered*. New York: G. W. Dillingham, Co., 1899.

The War of the Rebellion: A Compilation of the Official Records of the Union and Confederate Armies. Ser. I, Vol. XXVII, pts. 1, 2, 3. Washington, D.C.: Government Printing Office, 1880-1901.

Weigley, Russell F. *The American Way of War: A History of United States Military Strategy and Policy*. New York: Macmillan Publishing Co., Inc., 1973.

West, John C. *A Texan in Search of a Fight*. Waco, Tx.: J. S. Hill and Company, 1901.

Weygant, Charles H. *History of the One Hundred and Twenty-Fourth Regiment, N.Y.S.V.* Gaithersburg, Md.: Journal Printing House, 1877.

Winschel, Terrence J. "Their Supreme Moment: Barksdale's Brigade at Gettysburg." *Gettysburg Magazine*. 1 (July 1989), pp. 70-78.

Wilcox, Cadmus M. *Rifles and Rifle Practice*. New York: D. Van Nostrand, 1859.

Wiley, Bell Irvin. *The life of Billy Yank, the Common Soldier of the Union*. Indianapolis: Bobbs-Merrill, 1952.

_____. *The life of Johnny Reb, the Common Soldier of the Confederacy*. New York: Bobbs-Merrill, 1943.

Young, Jesse Bowman. *The Battle of Gettysburg*. Dayton, Ohio: Morningside Bookshop, 1976.

Index